Praise for *Abolitio*

T0023249

"In this powerful, wise, and well-crafted book, filled with insight and provocation, Angela Y. Davis, Gina Dent, Erica R. Meiners, and Beth E. Richie make it patently and abundantly clear why abolitionist feminism is necessary. Offering vivid snapshots from a political movement, the book explains how organizing to end violence without turning to violent institutions such as prisons and the police as remedies, is how we learn what we need to do to make change possible. Abolitionist feminists, they teach us, in taking up the slow, practical, and painstaking work of campaigning, also expand our political horizons and create imaginative tools for world building. Attentive to histories of organizing that are too quickly erased, and alive to new possibilities for working collectively in the present time, this book is as capacious and demanding as the abolitionist feminism it calls for. It gives us a name for what we want. Abolitionism. Now."

—**Sara Ahmed**, author of *Willful Subjects*

"Neither manifesto nor blueprint for revolution, this extraordinary book makes the most compelling case I've ever seen for the indivisibility of feminism and abolition, for the inseparability of gendered and state violence, domestic policing and militarism, the street, the home, and the world. Combining decades of analytical brilliance and organizational experience, Davis, Dent, Meiners, and Richie offer a genealogy of the movements that brought us here, lessons learned, battles won and lost, and the ongoing collective struggle to build a thoroughly revolutionary vision and practice. A provocation, an incitement, an offering, an invitation to a difficult struggle to which we must all commit. Now."

—**Robin D. G. Kelley**, author of *Freedom Dreams: The Black Radical Imagination*

ABOLITION. FEMINISM. NOW.

The Abolitionist Papers Series

Edited by Naomi Murakawa

Also in this series:

Change Everything: Racial Capitalism and the Case for Abolition
Ruth Wilson Gilmore

Rehearsals for Living
Robyn Maynard and Leanne Betasamosake Simpson

*We Do This 'Til We Free Us: Abolitionist Organizing
and Transforming Justice*
Mariame Kaba

ABOLITION. FEMINISM. NOW.

Angela Y. Davis, Gina Dent,
Erica R. Meiners, and Beth E. Richie

Haymarket Books
Chicago, Illinois

Published in 2022 by
Haymarket Books
P.O. Box 180165
Chicago, IL 60618
773-583-7884
www.haymarketbooks.org
info@haymarketbooks.org

ISBN: 978-1-642592-58-0

Distributed to the trade in the US through Consortium Book Sales and Distribution (www.cbsd.com) and internationally through Ingram Publisher Services International (www.ingramcontent.com).

This book was published with the generous support of Lannan Foundation and Wallace Action Fund.

Special discounts are available for bulk purchases by organizations and institutions. Please email info@haymarketbooks.org for more information.

Cover design by Abby Weintraub.

Printed in Canada by union labor.

Library of Congress Cataloging-in-Publication data is available.

10 9 8 7 6 5 4 3 2

CONTENTS

PREFACE

In 2001, a cluster of people attached to two emerging organizations connected to burgeoning movements gathered in a stuffy room over a weekend to hash out more than a statement. A key instigator for the small convening—primarily of women of color—was a pressing question: how to continue to knit together campaigns and analyses focused *both* on building a world without prisons and policing *and* building a world free of gender and sexual violence. INCITE! Women of Color Against Violence was a growing network challenging the mainstream/whitestream anti-violence movement's reliance on policing and punishment, and Critical Resistance had recently coalesced into an organization of abolitionists campaigning for the end of policing and prisons.[1] While both were new and developing networks with many overlapping people and shared analyses, these two groups recognized the value of articulating a collective vision and the importance of writing and circulating a statement on the difficult intersection of their shared work. They understood that crafting a joint statement that balanced an attention to both interpersonal and state violence represented not only an engagement with the thorniest subjects for both organizations but also an opportunity for public engagement in the production of shared analytics, campaign demands, and radical visions.

Members of the two newly formed groups spent an intense weekend at Mills College in Oakland, California, hammering out the "INCITE!-Critical Resistance Statement on Gender Violence and the Prison Industrial Complex," which clearly named the vision and the challenge.[2] The statement reads in part:

> It is critical that we develop responses to gender violence that do not depend on a sexist, racist, classist, and homophobic criminal justice system. It is also important that we develop strategies that challenge the criminal justice system and that also provide safety for survivors of sexual and domestic violence.

Outlining how "radical freedom, mutual accountability, and passionate reciprocity" can build toward "the survival and care of all peoples," this eleven-point statement identified at its core precisely why abolition must be feminist and why feminism must be abolitionist. Like most collaborative political work, the INCITE!-Critical Resistance Statement arrived in 2001 long past its due date and initially landed quietly. Originally published both as a poster and a manifesto, the statement circulated in feminist and abolitionist movement spaces, propelled by the clarity and compelling nature of its demands and the growing cadre of organizers with whom the statement resonated. As a key reference point in the history of abolition feminism, the document is heralded as an exemplary and clarion call for a more complex approach to anti-police and anti-prison movements, as well as an insistence on antiracism and anticapitalism as central dimensions of contemporary feminism.

In 2021, we return to this statement and its interventions at a critical moment for the future of social justice, as contemporary organizing makes abolition increasingly irresistible both as a mode of analysis and a political practice. Inching from the margins toward the mainstream, from the end of course syllabi to the beginning, calls for abolition proliferate. *Guardian* headlines announce "unprecedented" support for defunding the police. *Teen Vogue* publishes multiple articles, all identifiable with the tag *abolition*, on topics ranging from how police do not make us safer to why hate crime laws will not end anti-Asian violence.[3] Crowds in the street chant *Abolition*. The proliferation of abolitionist lawyering has been spurred in part by the National Lawyers Guild's resolution endorsing abolition in 2015, by formerly incarcerated people opening law offices like Pittsburgh's Abolitionist Law Center, and in webinars and organizing sponsored by groups such as Law for Black Lives. School boards from Oakland to Minneapolis are voting to cancel contracts with police departments. Colleges and universities are questioning the role of campus police and reconsidering contractual relationships with local law enforcement.

Yet as abolition becomes more influential as a goal, its collective feminist lineages are increasingly less visible, even during moments made possible precisely *because* of feminist organizing, especially that of young queer people of color whose pivotal labor and analysis is so often erased. As some recognized twenty years ago, abolition is most effectively advanced by naming and elevating an analysis and practice that is collective *and* feminist. We return to the profound intervention of the INCITE!-Critical

Resistance Statement: abolition is unimaginable without our radical, anticapitalist, antiracist, decolonial, queer feminism. This
small book argues that abolitionist traditions have relied on feminist analysis and organizing from their inception and that the
version of feminism we embrace is also not possible without an
abolitionist imagination. Bridging the overlapping but sometimes
discontinuous worlds of scholars and organizers, we explore recent movements and organizational formations—including those
anchored by INCITE! Women of Color Against Violence and
Critical Resistance—revealing an ecosystem of abolition feminism that is often relegated to the background. As freedom is a
constant struggle, abolition feminism has always been a politics—
the refusal to consign humans and other beings to disposability—
inseparable from practice.[4]

We look to the interventions offered by earlier feminist organizers. The Combahee River Collective Statement (1977), for example, was one of several key political treatises that established a
political path for radical feminist organizing and that functioned,
like all manifestos and open statements, as both a declaration and
a process.[5] While for many the Combahee River Collective Statement is a historical document establishing contemporary Black,
lesbian/queer, anticapitalist feminism, the organizing that shaped
its creation was as central as the content of the statement. Centering the lives of Black women and other women of color, their collective organizing generated a sense of urgency for the kind of truth
telling in which on-the-ground feminist campaigns for liberation
engaged deeply with larger, overarching political principles and
debates. This broad, optimistic, action-oriented, complex sense

of abolition feminism and its theory of change reverberates in the efforts of organizations that actively work to free people—like the Brisbane, Australia–based Sisters Inside and the UK's Sisters Uncut—and across contemporary statements, open letters, posters, and manifestos from networks like the Crunk Feminist Collective, the Movement for Black Lives, the Statement of Solidarity with Palestine from the Abolition and Disability Justice Coalition, and, of course, the INCITE!-Critical Resistance Statement.

We frame this book as a critical genealogy rather than a manifesto, one that emphasizes how important it is to trace political lineages. We offer a set of ideas and thick descriptions of unfinished practices rather than promoting rigid definitions. We attempt to reveal the common constitutive threads of the work and the promise of abolition feminism rather than constrain it to a sectarian political position. From storefronts in Chicago and prisons in Manchester to São Paulo streets and Johannesburg classrooms, our work proceeds genealogically to address subjugated histories of organizing that must inform and strengthen our present mobilizations. We use the term *ecosystem* to avoid a prescriptive or reifying framework and to amplify a dynamic ecology of political work, highlighting legacies, analytics, and questions often erased or obscured. We also use the term ecosystem to mark the complexity of a landscape populated with intertwined networks, campaigns, mobilizations, and organizations. Narrating a history of the present ecosystem—attending to subjugated knowledges and erasures—not only gestures to the underlying strata of necessary collective labor but also provides key imaginative and conceptual tools to engage with in our contemporary moment.

As our thinking and practice continues to be stretched and challenged by learning, teaching, and analyzing collective struggle, we do not offer this collaborative project as a thoroughgoing linear historical account of every organizational or conceptual treatment of abolition feminism. Instead, *Abolition. Feminism. Now.* puts abolition feminism as a concept into conversation with both the historical and contemporary ideological and political praxis that demands explicit and expansive ideas about how to go about freedom-making. As a critical genealogy, we start with a recognition that these overlapping histories of abolitionist and feminist movements are deeply intertwined, but they do not unfold alongside each other in neat chronological order. The historian Elsa Barkley Brown describes history as "everybody talking at once, multiple rhythms being played simultaneously" and reminds us that "a linear history will lead us to a linear politics and neither will serve us well in an asymmetrical world."[6] We welcome other renditions of abolition feminism, and we contend that genealogies should always be questioned, because there is always an unacknowledged reason for beginning at a certain moment in history as opposed to another, and it always matters which narratives of the present are marginalized or expunged. Rather than read this short book and the snapshots of campaigns, organizational formulations, and analyses we offer as a road map—as prescriptive tools for the present and future—or as the authoritative voice on organizations or movements, we suggest an engagement with the goal of our collective writing: to expand dialogue, practice, reflection, and more.

INTRODUCTION

Abolition. Feminism. Now.

Why Abolition Feminism

As abolition haltingly moves into public discourse and as some of its proponents underscore the feminist dimension of abolition as well as the abolitionist dimension of feminism, a clear articulation of the term *abolition feminism* becomes a critical challenge. Concepts, derived both from organizing and scholarship, can become brittle, empty terms—tools to wield against others—rather than living, generative, and rigorous frameworks that deepen and strengthen our theoretical understanding and our movements for social and political transformation.

When we began to collaborate on this book, we assumed that identifying what was and is feminist or abolitionist would be relatively simple. Yet this emerged as a more complex question, partially due to the medium: it can be challenging to write about organizing and ideas that are by nature in motion and therefore always nuanced in their relationality. Neither abolition nor feminism are static identifiers but rather political methods and practices. Is a project or a campaign feminist or abolitionist if participants do not use these words to describe their labor or campaign? Could we discretely mark what was "feminist" about "abolition" or "abolitionist" about "feminism"? How does abolition feminism take up the political questions that are germane but often obscured in the rendering of both concepts, considering racial capitalism, heteropatriarchy, internationalism, and transphobia as examples? Because these and other questions continue to play generative roles without demanding reductionist responses, we punctuate each word in the title with a full stop to signify that each of these concepts, with their own singular histories, frames this project. As abolition and feminism continue to be theorized discretely by a range of scholars and organizers, our project is not to erase, correct, or supplant these preexisting (and ongoing) efforts. Rather, the very meaning of the term *abolition feminism* incorporates a dialectic, a relationality, and a form of interruption: an insistence that abolitionist theories and practices are most compelling when they are also feminist, and conversely, a feminism that is also abolitionist is the most inclusive and persuasive version of feminism for these times.

While these approaches are always analytically and experientially overlapping—the movement to end gender and sexual violence, for example, can never be isolated from the work to end state violence, including the violence of policing—this more holistic understanding cannot always be assumed. As Critical Race Theorist Mari Matsuda wrote in 1991, a feminism that is able to meaningfully challenge emergent and existing forms of domination must always be flexible enough to "ask the other question":

> The way I try to understand the interconnection of all forms of subordination is through a method I call "ask the other question." When I see something that looks racist, I ask, "Where is the patriarchy in this?" When I see something that looks sexist, I ask, "Where is the heterosexism in this?" When I see something that looks homophobic, I ask, "Where are the class interests in this?" Working in coalition forces us to look for both the obvious and the nonobvious relationships of domination, and, as we have done this, we have come to see that no form of subordination ever stands alone.[1]

Matsuda's invocation requires an acknowledgement of the intersectionality of struggles and also represents our willingness to anticipate change and to build into our organizing a critical, generative reflexivity and opportunity to learn and grow.

For us, abolition feminism is political work that embraces this both/and perspective, moving beyond binary either/or logic and the shallowness of reforms. We recognize the relationality of state and individual violence and thus frame our resistance accordingly: supporting survivors and holding perpetrators accountable, working locally and internationally, building communities while responding to immediate needs. We work alongside people who are incarcerated while we demand their release. We mobilize in outrage against the rape of another woman and reject increased policing as the response. We support and build sustainable and long-term cultural and political shifts to end ableism and transphobia, while proliferating different "in the moment" responses when harm does happen. Sometimes messy and risky, these collective practices of creativity and reflection shape new visions of safety, animating complex landscapes that shape abolition feminism.

An ability to look both inward and outward, to meet both immediate demands and confront broad systems of injustice, and to think in complicated and layered ways about abolition represents a feminist approach to change. Our approach builds on notions of double and triple jeopardy put forth by Fran Beal and the Third World Women's Alliance, along with Deborah King's theory of multiple jeopardy or the idea that forms of domination and oppression both interrelate and compound—what Kimberlé Crenshaw would later define as intersectionality in the legal context.[2] These ideas have important lineages, often stretching back to the nineteenth century. Abolition feminism is a praxis—a politically informed practice—that demands intentional movement and insightful responses to the violence of systemic oppression. Building on these foundational approaches, this theory of change proclaims that we can and must do multiple things at the same time. We work locally and internationally. We hold people accountable and believe that people can change. We believe in being radical and active. We reflect, learn, and adjust our practices. We react to injustice. We build different ways of living. We are clear that organizing to end gender violence must include work against the prison industrial complex—against border patrols, against the incarceration of disability, against the criminalization of radical democratic protest—and as centrally, for mutual aid, cop-free schools, reproductive justice, and dignity for trans lives.[3] All this is possible because the "we" is not a set of individuals but rather a collective that grounds and defines its members and the projects, goals, and campaigns that are connected to the everyday, thus encompassing joy and struggle. Inextricably.

Abolition feminism does not shy away from contradictions, which are often the spark for change. Holding onto this both/and, we can and do support our collective immediate and everyday needs for safety, support, and resources while simultaneously working to dismantle carceral systems. Unhoused people should be afforded a safe place to sleep while we organize campaigns to build housing for all. Campaigns to close jails and prisons can move forward as we continue to teach classes inside prisons and as we support restorative justice processes and organize around parole hearings. Protests continue against sexual assault and murders committed by police officers while we build international solidarity movements against the exportation of militarized police tactics. Discovering and in fact embracing this ambiguous terrain located in the space between necessary responses to immediate needs and collective and radical demands for structural and ultimately revolutionary change is a hallmark of abolition feminism. Rather than being limitations, prescriptive horizons, or opportunities for empty quick fixes that resolve little, these contradictions are generative and necessary sites for collective analysis and labor.

The negotiation of this terrain also continues to create experimental and collective practices of safety, accountability, and healing untethered from the existing criminal legal system. Often named formally as community accountability or transformative justice, these tools and practices (with accompanying analysis) provide and proliferate responses without engaging the carceral or punitive state. Engagement is both reactive—what to do at the moment when harm and violence happen—and also provides examples and ideas for wider, longer-term preventative frameworks, or how to stop harm from happening. The practices of community accountability and transformative justice emanate from our political frameworks and offer multiple concrete ways for more people to become involved.

This growing and internationalist abolition feminist ecosystem—sustained overwhelmingly by unpaid labor—continues to produce radical tools and other resources. Before dissolving in January 2020, Berlin's Transformative Justice Kollektiv spent years documenting the multiple ways ordinary people try to respond to interpersonal harm, particularly gender and sexual violence, without resorting to police and prisons and offered workshops and resources to share tactics and strategies. With reading and learning circles, discussion groups, and other workshops, Alternative Justice in India works to offer "community-based, anti-carceral and feminist interventions to sexual harm and abuse in India." Through direct action, statements, and political education events, the United Kingdom's Sisters Uncut network concretely identifies and demands how budgetary resources can be removed from carceral forms and reinvested in communities, in health care, education, and the arts. Survived & Punished and Love & Protect support survivors who are criminalized for self-defense by developing campaigns that advocate for individuals, and they simultaneously make visible structural and systemic forms of state violence. Queer and trans networks—from the UK's Bent Bars group to the Bay Area's Transgender, Gender Variant and Intersex Justice Project—build and disseminate ways to guarantee safety, when calling the police is not an option, and when some are locked up in institutions predicated on violence.

Among this rich ecology of resources, "how-to" texts about practicing transformative justice and community accountability circulate and ignite discussion and practice, and spur further invention. People Against Prisons Aotearoa in Aotearoa/ New Zealand offers pamphlets to accompany their workshops, including "Transformative Justice Workshop: Practical Ways of Solving Interpersonal Harm and Conflict in our Communities," which provide tools to address everyday forms of conflict without engaging law enforcement.[4] *Fumbling Towards Repair* by Mariame Kaba and Shira Hassan is a "Workbook for Community Accountability Facilitators."[5] Ejeris Dixon and Leah Lakshmi Piepzna-Samarasinha's *Beyond Survival: Strategies and Stories from the Transformative Justice Movement* and the edited collection by Ching-In Chen and comrades entitled *The Revolution Starts at Home: Confronting Intimate Violence within Activist Communities* are full of stories reflecting on and analyzing how people are experimenting, sometimes unsuccessfully, with addressing conflict and harm within organizing communities.[6] The 576-page toolkit by Creative Interventions and the Story-Telling and Organizing Project in Oakland offer tools, language, and a wealth of material to begin to study, and to practice. Not a checklist or a one-stop fix, this expanding constellation of resources and organizations—one piece of our internationalist abolition feminist ecosystem—offers multiple, tangible tools for people to practice, together, now.[7] These resources—and too many others—are shared, critiqued, translated, and modified at grassroots convenings and gatherings across the globe, almost all organized by uncompensated labor.

Alongside these textual resources, artists continue to produce a range of visual interventions in our carceral state—including works that meticulously document the realities of day-to-day survival in prison. Artists have always been key agents seeding resistance and providing the tools for us to imagine otherwise—as exemplified by the visuals incorporated throughout this book. Our posters, memes, banners, statements, slogans, Signal and Snapchat groups, and more also create—to tweak a phrase from the visual arts scholar Nicole Fleetwood, an anti-"carceral aesthetics,"[8] or, as we would frame it, an abolition feminist aesthetics—to grow our collective capacities to visualize the regime of heterogendered and racialized punishment that is the US prison/police state and also the myriad ways that people—poor, queer, First Nations, brown, Black, and/or non-citizens—attempt to flourish and resist in spite of all of these obstacles. Over the past decade the audience has also exploded for the work of writers who center speculative Black female (and queer) futures such as Octavia Butler, N. K. Jemison, and Nnedi Okorafor. The growth of interest in these authors and artists who center the struggle for Black futurity—and the increasingly wide body of work that has emerged in dialogue with these speculative texts—cannot be separated from the material demands that emerged during this time period: Fund Black Futures.[9] Abolition. Feminism. Now. While local organizing continues to transform the discursive environment, furthering and legitimizing abolitionist-oriented discourse on prisons and policing, cultural and artistic projects also help to denaturalize the carceral state and to frame this institutionalized violence as an essential topic for mainstream discussions. Consider, for example,

Illustration of sci-fi's kindling of radical imagination by Ira M. Leigh, 2015.

Papel Machete's multimedia puppetry performance that creates a speculative narrative about the last prison in the US.[10] Visual culture, music, art, and fiction shape the popular imagination in profound ways, outpacing changes in policy and law.

Yet, as all these resources acknowledge, even as we create multiple interventions and responses to supplant carceral approaches—some formally named transformative justice and some not—harm will occur. Women will be sexually assaulted, trans people will be beaten, disabled people will be held hostage in their households, and Black and other people of color will hurt each other. Our work is not to pretend these forms of violence will not happen. Our own contexts, projects, worksites, and organizing are not immune. As we write, allegations of sexual harm, transphobia, and racism unfold in organizations and movements around us. We struggle. And we recognize that the highest costs are often experienced by those most vulnerable: people living and organizing, without pay, from within prisons and other carceral sites and those working, without pay, in movements and grassroots organizations. With humility we acknowledge these risks, and yet we dive in, together. This is not impossible work because we do this together. *Abolition. Feminism. Now.* outlines how and why abolition is unimaginable without feminism, how feminism is unimaginable without abolition, and why this dialogue is imperative, now. We hope that readers will reflect on the ideas in this book and let themselves be moved to action—action not prescribed by us but inspired by the work, the ideas, and the challenges archived in this book.

Why Us

Collective abolition feminist organizing, teaching, and learning bring us together. As scholars, educators, and organizers, we are involved in projects that revolve around prison and police abolition, as we attempt to grow anti-carceral approaches within feminist anti-violence movements. Collaboratively, we have built and supported a number of organizations, worked on campaigns, participated in delegations, convened gatherings, learned (and taught), all as part of the work of movements and organizing. In particular we have ongoing and deep histories with INCITE! Women, Gender Non-Conforming, and Trans People of Color Against Violence and Critical Resistance. Angela is one of the founding members of Critical Resistance, Beth is a founding member of INCITE!, Gina has been involved in Critical Resistance since its inception and first conference in 1998, and Erica joined Critical Resistance in 2006. For Beth, Gina, and Angela, these exchanges began in the late 1990s, with Erica, the youngest in our collaborative effort, joining ten years later. In car rides and on panels, in organizing meetings and campaigns, in classrooms and strategy sessions, over meals in kitchens, these fragments of conversations moved across Chicago, New York, Oakland, Bahia, Brisbane, London, Palestine, and other parts of the globe. What does it mean that abolition now appears at the start of many syllabi as a foundation rather than an afterthought covered in a few weeks at the end of a course? What is the impact of few people formally recognizing how feminism has shaped abolition? Why must we keep agitating to ensure that feminism is informed by abolition?

Our decision to collaborate on a small book entitled *Abolition. Feminism. Now.* was made long before the spring 2020 antiracist protests and uprisings in the United States and around the world and the emergence and strengthening of demands such as "Defund the Police" and "Police Out of Schools." We met by Zoom weekly before Zoom classes, conferences, and other online gatherings became the norm. We continued through the early days of the pandemic, during uprisings that unfolded on our blocks, and while negotiating changing working, living, and organizing conditions. We persisted through domestic unpredictability, insufficient bandwidth, tornados, new puppies, forest fires, caregiving demands, mandated shelter in place orders, and even a white supremacist insurrection. Our calls were punctu-ated by the urgency of the now—check-ins about the health of loved ones, real-time updates on pressing local actions, questions about teaching and learning, worries about the 2020 election, and strategy sessions about movement weaknesses and futures. This project has always felt imperative: our involvement in multiple communities that simultaneously resist both imprisonment and gender violence illustrates the imperative of an indivisibility—feminism is central to abolition and abolition is indivisible from our feminism—motivating us to collaborate to document, the-orize, and amplify abolition feminism. The mobilizations of 2020, the white supremacist insurrection of early 2021, and the COVID-19 pandemic have only heightened this urgency and yet also imposed multiple competing demands.

As the landscape surrounding this project continued to rapid-ly shift and as the work started and stopped according to everyday demands, we paid careful attention to a collaborative process. We come from very different locations, were trained across divergent academic and organizing traditions, and work and teach in inter-secting but also varying domains. Perhaps unintentionally, our writing practice for this project reflected the organizing we aimed to engage and in part to chronicle. We sought a collective voice that reflected our shared thinking and practice, nurtured an on-going critical reflexivity, and we worried about what and who was missed or left out, always mindful of the imperative to acknowl-edge narratives, people, and analytics easily forgotten or buried. We struggled through dissatisfaction with the technologies and tools available to support collective writing and analysis, embraced generative curiosities from overlapping and also discordant tools and vocabularies, while maintaining our deep sense of accountability to collective mobilizations—past, present, and future. We made explicit a commitment to unfinished discussions about our imagined audience's knowledges, as well as our collective desire to do more than simply chronicle present history and gesture toward the work and the futures to come, working with humility and a profound recognition that collectives incorporating difference rather than individual actors propel and sustain us. These modes of productive convergence and dissonance are laced throughout our writing and also reflected in the movements and mobilizations chronicled. Our key point of unity is an ongoing commitment to the practice and the politics of abolition feminism and a trust engendered from sharing labors, visions, lessons, spaces, and care over the last decade(s). This is the always slow time of collectivity, urgent and ungainly, deliberate and wholly in.

Why Collective

Key to this abolition feminist ecosystem are networks, organizations, and collectives. This work is never a solo project. Individuals tire, fade. Movements deepen and continue. Sometimes the group is only a few folks working together in a church basement, but these gatherings, networks, and ad hoc or formal groups create insurgent sites of political education that build relationships, share language, strategy, tools, and analysis, and create openings for people to learn and to practice: *what tools are available to hold someone accountable if we don't call the police?* Collectivism is a throughline across generations, peoples, and mobilizations—undervalued and unrecognized but key to freedom-making.

We are careful here not to romanticize any network or campaign. People do the labor and therefore it, like all of us, is always flawed. And a turn to "the community" is fraught, sometimes mythic: community is at once a radical vision, a fugitive possibility, and a struggle—abolition feminism in practice. The networks and collectives represented in this genealogy (only a fraction of the emergent work across the abolitionist feminist landscape) remind us that abolition will not end all harm or interpersonal violence: we must do the work to both prevent and reduce harm, while we practice and grow transformative ways to respond when harm does happen. Abolition feminism is this intentional investment of our resources to support a flourishing of our collective best selves, while reclaiming "accountability" from the carceral regime.

Collective organizing is always about learning and change, and we know the risks are borne unevenly. And while a recognition of the complexity of standpoint epistemology does not cosign learned ignorance—for example cisgender and/or white people whose fragility and incompetence is the result of a willful commitment to not knowing, not listening, or not learning—political consciousness is an ongoing, collective, and pedagogical process rather than a finish line. Yet how do we cultivate movement spaces for people to learn, to be wrong and unlearn, and to be accountable and change? As this work can only happen in relation, in communities, it is always imperative that the burden of labor does not again fall on the same bodies—notably women, usually women of color.

Our ability to ask the other question and to struggle and practice collectively is both strengthened and made more difficult because the aspirations of abolition feminism are often described as utopian. Abolition is by necessity speculative, and we ardently embrace its utopian dimension.[11] Yet if a movement is framed as a progression toward utopia, its conceptual and organizing moves can also reinforce a central myth about abolition: that it is impractical, unattainable, a dream. (The framing of the US as the dystopic and exceptional outlier on an international carceral state spectrum does not help to erode feelings of the impossibility of abolition in the US with a concurrent minimization of the necessity for abolition in other nation-states.) Utopian approaches can be cast as limited, and it is a refrain too often leveled against abolitionists, along with our "evangelical zeal," our naivete, our failure to be pragmatic, and our extremism.[12]

Our intervention is to reground ourselves in the inseparability of feminism from abolition and to insist that not only is it critical to make space for what we have not yet been able to imagine, but at the same time to amplify that the practice is grounded, everyday, and already unfolding—now. Vision and practice are not contradictory but are rather inseparable, the insistent prefiguration of the world we know we need. As one of the starters of the No One Is Illegal movement, Harsha Walia writes: "Prefiguration is the notion that our organizing reflects the society we wish to live in—that the methods we practice, institutions we create, and relationships we facilitate within our movements and communities align with our ideals."[13]

The organizations referenced in this project, and the many

more in neighborhoods across the globe, form a dynamic constellation shaped by and through abolition feminism that circulates and deploys everyday tools to end our reliance on policing and punishment and create more authentically safe communities.

A *now* practice, abolition feminism refuses to let go of the visionary—that which does not yet exist—and the radicalness of the imaginary as a space for what is yet unthinkable, at the edge of the possible. We say yes to Octavia Butler's brilliant speculativeness: we will dream our way out; we must imagine beyond the given. We also say yes to the daily practice of organizers such as Fannie Lou Hamer and Fay Honey Knopp: do the work, every day, any way. And as our beloved now deceased comrade Rose Braz noted in a 2008 interview, "A prerequisite to seeking any social change is the naming of it. In other words, even though the goal we seek may be far away, unless we name it and fight for it today, it will never come."[14] The productive tension of holding onto a radical, real, and deep vision while engaging in the messy daily practice *is* the feminist praxis: the work of everyday people to try, to build, to make. And this requires collectivity. Always.

Why *Now.*

Abolition feminism *is* our political moment. After the racist execution carried out in Minneapolis, Minnesota, by uniformed representatives of state power and recorded on cell phones by bystanders, the name of George Floyd echoed around the world. How also to echo the murders and ongoing assaults on Asian and Asian American women, or the violent arrests of Black trans peo-

Demands put forward in 2020 by the #8toAbolition campaign, aimed toward dismantling systems of state violence.

ple, the detention of Latinx and other immigrant children at "the border," or the disappearance of women in Ciudad Juárez, Mexico? Even though for the first time in our memory, officials almost immediately declared the police killing of George Floyd to be a "murder" and the mass murder of Asian women in Atlanta in 2021 to be a "hate crime," the collective awakening was occasioned by the fact that tens of millions and perhaps more witnessed the last nine minutes of George Floyd's life and the clear targeting of Asian women.[15] Even for those who may be unfamiliar with the history of racist violence in the United States, these scenes aroused the historical specter of lynching and femicide. But this time, we were all implicated. And to fail to respond was tantamount to implicit assent. As we prepare this manuscript for publication, like the vast numbers of protesters and those sympathizing with activists in the streets throughout the world, we are still reeling from the sense that historical time has fast-forwarded, even as the present illuminates how much we are still held captive by unresolved questions from the past.

This collective moment has been ushered in through a long trajectory of campaigns, mobilizations, and actions, often precipitated by violence and death. Although we know the names of vast numbers of Black men who have lost their lives to police violence, the women, gender nonconforming people, trans people, and sex workers who are killed are most often relegated to the background. During the period preceding the murder of George Floyd, Breonna Taylor, a young Black woman who worked as an emergency medical technician, was executed by police in Louisville, Kentucky, as they entered her residence on a no-knock warrant apparently issued because she was a prior acquaintance of a person sought by the police. Breonna Taylor was in bed with her boyfriend when the police broke into her house and shot her eight times. If the name of George Floyd summons an unending list of Black men who have been targets of racist state violence—in the most recent era, Mike Brown, Eric Garner, Freddie Gray, Walter Scott, Philando Castile, and many others—the names of women are often erased, with the exceptions of Breonna Taylor, Sandra Bland, Rekia Boyd, and a few others.

George Floyd's murder became a major catalyst for abolitionist demands in large part because of prior radical organizing. In 2012, just days after her twenty-first birthday, CeCe McDonald was arrested for defending herself against racist and transphobic street violence. As she faced a charge of murdering her attacker and a lengthy prison sentence, a small but significant queer, trans, and mostly young multiracial network raised the visibility of her case through social media and organized street actions and workshops. This support was especially important during the nineteen months CeCe, a Black trans woman, was being held in a men's prison. CeCe and the campaign that emerged around her also worked to name all the ways the criminal legal system serves as an apparatus of repression against people on the peripheries of society, particularly trans people of color. This organizing surrounding CeCe, almost a decade before the summer 2020 uprising, elucidated the ideological connections between state violence, street violence, and interpersonal violence, a conjunction at the heart of all of the work of abolition feminism.

Campaigns centering Black women who are the targets of the interlocking forms of interpersonal and state violence have emerged in the US, as they have in the rest of the imprisoned world, where race, gender, and marginality play a similar role in criminalization. On January 11, 2016, Sarah Reed, a thirty-two-year-old Black woman with a history of psychiatric disability, became the last woman to die in London's Holloway Prison (the largest women's prison in Western Europe until it was permanently closed six months later). Sarah was found dead in her cell with strips of linen around her neck. She was on remand in Holloway after having been charged with grievous bodily harm because she had attempted to defend herself from sexual assault by a patient in the secure unit of a mental health facility. Although the inquest found that her death was self-inflicted, officials were not persuaded that she actually intended to take her own life. The failure to provide adequate and timely care, and her incarceration in lieu of appropriate health care, were both causal factors in what was ruled a suicide. In the aftermath of this death-in-custody, Sisters Uncut, an antiracist and feminist direct action group that organizes against cuts to domestic violence services, occupied the Visitor's Center at Holloway in memory of Sarah Reed and the ten other women who had died in Holloway since 2004, demanding that this space of state violence be transformed into a building providing anti-violence services for women and nonbinary people.

While all of us have been involved in many such cases, the temporalities of our struggles were shattered during this period. What we understand as real time changed in drastic ways during the time that we were working on this book. As noted, the original idea was brewing for years: originating during our discussions at conferences, over meals at events, while reading books together and thinking through campaign strategies, during long drives to meet with our students in courses that we teach at Stateville prison. Inspired by the exciting ways that feminist and abolitionist ideas are converging to enliven resistance movements, now appeared to be the right time to document this work.

The title of our book—*Abolition. Feminism. Now.*—reflects these feminist theories and practices in many parts of the world that acknowledge, like Sisters Uncut, the CeCe McDonald cam-

Artwork by Micah Bazant, created in 2013 as part of the campaign to free CeCe McDonald.

paign, and the movement for justice for Breonna Taylor and others, the multiple ways in which struggles against individual and intimate violence are integrally tied to struggles against state violence. Across the globe, forms of resistance to state violence accentuate the historical and contemporary entanglements of systems of oppression. The work, for example, of Rio de Janeiro councilmember Marielle Franco, a queer, feminist, antiracist organizer assassinated in March 2018, who passionately challenged the militarization of Brazilian police forces, has deeply inspired many of us engaged in similar work in the United States. Marielle Franco's feminist approach and her articulation of race and gender made it absolutely clear that the defense of Black women must be linked to the struggle against police violence even when its immediate targets are predominantly male. Her organizing centered the needs of Black women in the city's favelas, including fighting for "nighttime nurseries" for working mothers and for reproductive rights for women, and articulated the conditions of poverty, militarization, violence, and repression to the structural and institutional impact of race and gender. Those who are attempting to radicalize electoral politics have been further emboldened by the fact that in the aftermath of Marielle's assassination an unprecedented number of Black women ran for office in Brazil, often referred to as the seeds of Marielle (*semillas de Marielle*): Erica Malunguinho da Silva, for example, became the first Black trans woman to be elected to the São Paulo legislative assembly.

US-centric discourses and organizing can saturate contemporary abolitionist political movements, reinforcing and deepening US imperialism and potentially eliding local histories of violence and resistance. Thus, internationalist engagements are imperative to illustrate the continuing and global repercussions of colonialism and imperialism embedded in police and carceral institutions. In 2020, in the context of a global #BlackLivesMatter insurgency, a South African collective published an action report, *Reimagining Justice in South Africa beyond Policing*. Highlighting the long history of the violence of incarceration and policing in South Africa (the collective, CopsAreFlops, has maintained that the South African Police Service purportedly kills three times more people per capita than US police forces), the report noted: "It is not about fitting a 'South African' narrative into an 'American' narrative . . . we are fundamentally having the same conversation."[16] By asserting that police violence in different places can be understood as different facets of the "same conversation," as CopsAreFlops suggests, we develop more capacious analytical approaches as our strategies and the ranks of our struggles expand.

Local mobilizations have global tentacles. For example, campaigns to challenge the militarization of US police have often focused attention on the Israeli army's role to train police departments around the world (including the very small force in Ferguson, Missouri). In the San Francisco Bay Area, Critical Resistance, the Arab Resource and Organizing Center, Xicana Moratorium Coalition, and other organizations led a protracted campaign that eventually caused the termination of Urban Shield, the weapons expo and SWAT training program that took place annually on September 11, attracting law enforcement agencies from throughout the world—including from the state of Israel. This campaign reflected shifts from positions that simply call for "more humane" police practices without changing existing law enforcement structures toward a more complex understanding of the way local police departments are affected by and in turn

Cover artwork by Mikayla Boorany for *Reimagining Justice in South Africa beyond Policing*, 2020.

strengthen tendencies toward militarization. Thus the 2019 victory in the campaign to stop Urban Shield represented not only a local win but a significant moment in the forging of internationalist approaches toward state violence.

This internationalism can help trace and build a vibrant and complex genealogy, reminding us to think beyond what constitutes the given within particular geopolitical contexts. The goal is not to aspire to any of these conditions: furloughs from prison for people serving long sentences is not an end goal. Yet an internationalist lens at least does the needed work to jar us out of familiar, everyday horizons and build analyses, linkages, and organizing. For example, recognizing that those in Montreal and London are involved in the same conversation as our South African counterparts strengthens our capacity to argue that policing can be driven by structural racism even when the majority of police officers are Black people. Perhaps one of the most compelling examples can be found in the work of the newly formed Palestinian Feminist Collective-Action Network and its radical commitment to anticolonialism and life-affirming decolonization in the face of Zionist violence. These and other opportunities to learn from organizing beyond our own violent borders also function as reminders that current arrangements are historically produced and can therefore be altered and that racial capitalism, like COVID-19, holds no fidelity to any nation-state.[17]

Because abolition feminism is a politics and a practice, we have structured this book around short chapters that offer snapshots from our collective and individual practices, campaigns, projects, learnings, and engagements. To illustrate the indivisibility of the core concepts that structure this book, chapter one offers a critical partial genealogy of abolition with feminist inflections, while chapter two provides a critical partial genealogy of anti-violence feminist movements with abolitionist inflections. Chapter three engages the specifics of one site, Chicago, to map how in this moment abolition feminism lives on the ground in neighborhoods, organizations, community groups, campaigns, and popular education initiatives that are working against carcerality and for freedom. None of the examples contained in this short project are finite, but we offer them to show how amid profound structural oppression and violence, there are spaces of possibility where imagination and creativity can thrive. Taken together, the examples in this book—a fraction of an emergent ecology—form a mosaic of what is made possible by abolition feminism, not in a prescriptive sense but rather to show that a new world is possible: already we are collectively building one.

⚜

We name the change we want: Abolition. Feminism. Now.

Abolition requires profound shifts in how we organize against oppression and what we do to create the world we want. For us, feminism offers a political and ideological map to guide that work. The urgency, the "now," is propelled by the recent uprisings across the US and the long history of daily struggles in Black, brown, immigrant, queer, and Indigenous communities— struggles for safety, for food justice, for a guaranteed just wage, and to expand the right to vote, as well as freedom from forced sterilization or gender assignment surgery and from repressive regimes of surveillance, control, and punishment. Importantly, while the urgency—the now—is animated by the murders of George Floyd, Breonna Taylor, and Marielle Franco, the rich legacy of abolition feminist organizing shapes today's struggles and reminds us of the slow work, in always urgent times, of building flourishing communities for the long haul.

MARIELLE PRESENTE

Poster from the ongoing struggle against the far right in Brazil by
Luciane Fortuna, Marielle Franco Instituto Collection.

I.

Abolition.

When the New York Women's House of Detention opened in 1932, it was heralded as a national model, an important example of "modern penology." Located in Greenwich Village where Sixth Avenue, Tenth Street, and Greenwich Avenue intersect, and constructed at a cost of two million dollars, this new prison was designed to address the increasing number of women entering the criminal legal system. News coverage emphasized a pivotal shift in the official vocabulary, mandating that the women incarcerated there be referred to as "inmates" instead of "prisoners," thus marking what were considered at the time to be significant reforms. The Women's House of Detention was also praised for its incorporation of emergent "scientific research," particularly the practice of carceral isolation as a response to the assumption that one of the "leading causes of crime" was the "ease with which young offenders become influenced by older law-breakers in prison." In what has become a familiar echo, building an "innovative" new prison in line with the "best" emerging science was framed as the necessary and most developed idea of reform.[1]

Yet despite the prison's goal of isolation, its nearness to the street and to the core of the city created tangible pathways for communication and exchange. Visitations by people inhabiting the "free world" were not always confined to officially sanctioned meetings inside the prison via telephone and through the small and eventually degraded plexiglass panes, which required both parties to remain standing for the duration of the visit. There were also decidedly unsanctioned street visits during which people screamed up from Greenwich Avenue calling upon anyone inside who happened to be listening to ask the person they wanted to visit to come to her window. Audre Lorde described this communication strategy in 1982:

> Information and endearments flew up and down, the conversants apparently oblivious to the ears of the passersby as they discussed the availability of lawyers, the length of stay, family, conditions, and the undying quality of true love. The Women's House of Detention, right smack in the middle of the Village, always felt like one up for our side—a defiant pocket of female resistance, ever-present as a reminder of possibility, as well as punishment.[2]

Because its proximity to the street provided access to communication that was unregulated and to a great extent unsurveilled by the prison, it also created conduits for organizing. However temporal and fractured, inside and outside organizers found ways to interrupt and destabilize the prison's regimes of isolation. In 1969, during the days between Christmas and the new year, the emergent Gay Liberation Front protested for twenty-four hours a day in front of the prison in response to the incarceration of Afeni

Shakur and Joan Bird—two Black Panthers whose cases attracted substantial media attention.

During the time Angela Davis spent in the House of D., as it was nicknamed, supporters helped to organize a bail campaign that was coordinated in part through this unregulated communication between the incarcerated and the streets. Prefiguring the Black Mamas Bail Out Action campaign initiated in 2017 by Mary Hooks of Southerners on New Ground (SONG), those on the outside raised money for bail, and women on the inside collectively decided who would benefit from the bail campaign.[3] There were women who spent many months behind bars even though their charges were relatively minor, because they and their family members outside had few or no resources. From their perspective, a bail set at $500 might as well have been $500,000. The organizing and collective decision-making among the imprisoned women was especially important because those who got out on bail committed to raising funds for the bail campaign after their release. While the mission of isolation was supported by what was presented as scientific evidence, literally concretizing the "modern" penology that the House of D. symbolized, the history of this institution was also always characterized by resistance.

The collective practices established by people inside and outside of the House of D. emerged from the tools and resources at hand—voices, people, money raised. While not explicitly named as abolitionist or often even as feminist, these collective practices are nevertheless important elements in the genealogy of abolition feminism. While bail funds had been created for political prisoners like H. Rap Brown, most incarcerated people did not have access to these networks. However, as far as we can determine, the campaign at the House of D. was one of the earliest instances of bail campaigns for people with no public profile—like the contemporary Black Mamas Bail Out Action and the emergence of grassroots bail bond funds across the United States.[4] The establishment of bail funds, the communication networks developed from shouting up to cell windows from the street, and the willful and collective refusal by those inside and outside to acquiesce in the isolation en-

Black Mamas Bail Out Action image designed by Micky Jordan for Mother's Day in 2019.

acted by the prison constituted a powerful early abolition feminist intervention. Current efforts to abolish bail altogether—such as the 2020 announcement by San Francisco district attorney Chesa Boudin that his office was terminating cash bail—owe a great deal to these earlier abolition feminist efforts.

In 1974, the population of the Women's House of Detention was moved to Rikers Island prison. The House of D. was demolished. Joan Nestle suggests that imprisoned women's persistent interruptions to the daily life of Greenwich Village streets, considered "bad for real estate and tourism," eventually prompted the mayor to close the prison.[5] After significant organizing, a garden was created on the former site of the House of D. These rich organizing histories have been largely scrubbed from abolitionist movement histories. Yet the emptiness of the 1932 argument for modern penology echoes in contemporary calls to create so-called kinder, nicer jails across the US, particularly in New York City, during struggles over an alternative plan to the now-delegitimized Rikers Island prison.

San Francisco, Denver, Bellingham, Los Angeles, and many other cities and counties are organizing against and sometimes successfully defeating proposed new jail (and prison) constructions, expansions, and associated financing schemes. Inconceivable to many even ten years ago, jail closure, the elimination of money bond, clemency, and "compassionate release" are now debated in mainstream media outlets such as the *Washington Post* and lauded in progressive public policy forums as examples of necessary change. These ideological and material shifts represent enormous gains. Yet an abolition feminist lens teaches us that our work is not simply about "winning" specific campaigns but reframing the terrain upon which struggle for freedom happens. Indeed, one of the fundamental precepts of abolition is that winning a campaign is not the only measure of success: *how* we struggle, how our work enables future struggles, and how we stay clear about what we are fighting for matters. Working from this snapshot of the generative analysis and histories of people organizing for liberation around and within the House of D., this chapter offers one pathway for thinking about how abolitionist practice was shaped by feminism. Incorporating the organizational formation of Critical Resistance and other networks that built contemporary abolitionist movements, the influence of the historical insights of W. E. B. Du Bois, and analysis from contemporary campaigns, this chapter traces the feminist throughlines propelling abolitionist practice. Today, as always, it is crucial to highlight these forms of organizing in a genealogy of abolition and feminism.

Organizing Genealogies

Three years before the demolition of the House of D., the Attica Brothers issued in 1971 a passionate call for abolition during the four-day rebellion that echoed across various movements and activist circles.[6] In the wake of the Attica uprising, numerous examples of the beginnings of a counterhegemonic discourse surfaced—such as the uprising at Walpole Prison in Massachusetts where incarcerated people organized a labor union in a prison and ran the prison[7]—even as this momentum was unfortunately soon hindered by the reigning law-and-order rhetoric. The American Friends Service Committee published *Struggle for Justice: A Report on Crime and Punishment in America.* The concluding section of this report emphasized, among other issues, "opposition to the construction of new prisons." The report argued that

> As a reform, "modern" prisons may relieve the harsher physical hardships of doing time, but the essential punitive element of prison—deprivation of liberty and free choice—remains. When pressures for reform lead to demands to relieve "overcrowding" by adding new cell or bed space, the result is inevitable: the coercive net of the justice system will be spread over a larger number of people, entrapping them for longer periods of time. If prisons are overcrowded, ways should be found to cut back the mass of criminal laws and the types of enforcement that send so many people to prison. The construction of new prisons is not compatible with our view of the proper role of criminal law in a democratic society.[8]

The 1976 handbook for abolitionists *Instead of Prisons* likewise clearly outlined strategies for decarceration and documented an abbreviated history of abolitionist analysis with more than a century of citations from incarcerated and free individuals and organizations. The handbook cited Judge Bruce M. Wright, who eventually served on the New York State Supreme Court, and who visited Greenhaven Prison in 1975: "For years I have condemned the prisons of America. I have always said that the prison system as it exists in America today, should be abolished. As I have grown older, I have seen no reason to change that view."[9] *Instead of Prisons* was coauthored by the Quaker activist Fay Honey Knopp, a groundbreaking twentieth-century abolitionist, who later argued that abolition was a significant dimension of radical feminism.[10]

These ideas were taken up in the 1970s by the Santa Cruz Women's Prison Project, which worked to create a vibrant community of people inside and outside prisons along the West Coast by hosting discussions on "alternatives to prison," circulating newsletters with shared updates and analysis, creating support networks for people inside and after release, and generating sustained campaigns to halt construction of new jails and prisons.[11] These contributions to the counterhegemonic discourse that emerged after Attica reveal a necessary core of abolition feminism already present in past efforts.

Abolitionist ideas about democracy, freedom, safety, and justice continued to percolate throughout the following decades, even as demands for substantive reform gave way to calls for increasingly punitive strategies often couched in the very reforms designed to render incarceration more humane. Almost twenty-five years after the demolition of the House of D., when the establishment of these early, site-specific forms of resistance—including grassroots bail funds—were largely forgotten, abolition as an idea was revivified by the 1998 conference "Critical Resistance: Beyond the Prison Industrial Complex." Drawing from earlier lineages, this convening offered abolitionism as a twenty-first-century strategy for addressing not only the staggering rise in the numbers of incarcerated people in the US but also increasingly in Europe, Australia, Africa, and South America. In the fall of 1996, Cassandra Shaylor, then a graduate student in History of Consciousness at UC Santa Cruz (UCSC) and an attorney for incarcerated women, and Angela Da-

Poster featuring artwork by Rupert Garcia, created for the 1998 Critical Resistance conference.

vis, faculty member in that department, first discussed the possibility of organizing a conference that would bring people together to develop radical anti-prison organizing strategies.[12] In order to avoid exceptionalizing those who could not afford to pay, admission to the conference was free, and additional funds were raised to support travel for formerly incarcerated people. It is worth noting that of the twenty-eight members of the organizing committee, all except five were women or nonbinary. Originally, organizers of the conference assumed that they were being optimistic in their expectations that several hundred activists from around the country could be persuaded to attend. However, by the time the actual conference took place in September 1998 at the University of California, Berkeley, some 3,500 were in attendance.

This gathering marked the beginning of an entirely new phase of anti-prison activism. It consolidated a major organizing presence, highlighting abolitionist approaches in cities like Oakland, New York, Chicago, New Orleans, Los Angeles, and Portland that involved such work as systematically challenging the construction of new prisons and promoting decarceration strategies. The group worked with educators to develop campaigns around such demands as "schools not jails" and "education not incarceration." Two-and-a-half years later, in May 2001, Critical Resistance was established as a national organization with Rose Braz as the campaign and media director. Today, after more than two decades of protests, campaigns, advocacy, and movement building, Critical Resistance has not only helped to direct public attention toward the prison crisis but also mobilized a wide swath of organizers who shifted the discourse away from liberal demands for prison reform toward prison abolition, recognizing that the same logic applies to structures of policing and other carceral formations. As a key moment in the history and genealogy of abolition, the convening marked the beginning of a movement philosophically anchored by the notion of abolition with strong feminist inflections.

The CR conference created a pathway for multiple other gatherings that propelled abolition. Some of these convenings—too many to chronicle—were singular events. For example, the 2007 conference "Transforming Justice: Ending the Criminalization and Imprisonment of Transgender and Gender Non-Conforming People" (organized and sponsored by the Transgender, Gender Variant and Intersex Justice Project, the Sylvia Rivera Law Project, Critical Resistance, and other organizations) demonstrated why analyses of the prison industrial complex that failed to account for queer and trans resistance are incomplete and inadequate.[13] Other gatherings became yearly opportunities for assessment integral to movement building: in March 2020, the tenth annual Beyond the Bars conference took place in New York, "Freedom Plans: Strategies for Challenging a Carceral Society," organized by a network of formerly incarcerated people, led by Kathy Boudin and Cheryl Wilkins. Yet other meetings shaped new organizations: in 2011 the abolitionist organization Students Against Mass Incarceration was founded at Howard University during the unfortunately unsuccessful campaign to save Troy Davis from the death penalty. After holding a national conference in 2013, drawing students from Historically Black Colleges and Universities like Morgan State, numerous campus-based campaigns emerged, such as the movement demanding divestment from private prisons.

Critical Resistance popularized radical analyses of the ways in which imprisonment and policing, firmly linked to developments in global capitalism, simultaneously incorporate and mask structural racism. This abolitionist movement sought to explain the tremendous increase in the numbers of imprisoned people during the 1980s in relation to the structural changes produced by the rise of global capitalism during that period. The

Poster created for the Critical Resistance ten-year-anniversary conference in Oakland, California, in 2008 by Pete Railand.

deindustrialization of the US economy, which led to the elimination of vast numbers of jobs, especially in heavy manufacturing like steel, auto, and mining, had a devastating impact on Black communities in cities like Detroit, Los Angeles, Philadelphia, and Chicago. Because the rise of global capitalism also involved neoliberal strategies to disestablish services associated with the welfare state, unemployed people lost any vestiges of a safety net. Instead of directly addressing problems created by structural shifts in the economy, the stopgap "solution" of punishment consolidated the link between racism and criminalization.

This movement was also shaped by organizing, especially by Black feminists, that continued to illuminate the punishing power of state programs marked as welfare and other social services. The existing welfare program Aid to Families with Dependent Children was associated within popular discourse with Black women, even as the majority of recipients were white. The myth of the Black "welfare queen" created an easy target and was a pivotal discursive strategy that held women responsible for criminal behavior in both the putative misuse of welfare funds and as generators of a culture of crime that would be largely perpetuated by their male children.[14] As Dorothy Roberts documented in *Killing the Black Body*, first published in 1997, "A persistent objective of American social policy has been to monitor and restrain this 'corrupting tendency' of Black motherhood."[15] Although child and family services are often misconceived as "soft" forms of surveillance and policing, what Roberts has called the "family regulation system," and more recently "the family policing system," is directly weaponized against poor families, disproportionately Black and Indigenous women.[16] Far from a "kind and just parent," state intervention re-sults in grotesque outcomes for families, particularly young folks.

What differentiates this explicitly abolitionist approach from prevailing ideas and scenarios addressing prison repression—both then and now—is the tenacious critique of prison reform and of criminal justice reform more broadly, as well as the recognition that the ideological impulse to contain all efforts to address the so-cial damage wrought by prisons within the parameters of "reform" serves to further authorize incarceration as the legitimate and im-mutable foundation of justice. Abolitionist organizing recognized that there were no easy reformist solutions to the hegemonic notion that Indigenous and Black people, other people of color, poor peo-ple, trans people, and women of all racial backgrounds who do not conform to dominant gender expectations were naturally inclined to criminality and belong in prison. An amalgam of economic, po-litical, cultural, and representational forces produces this fatal "nor-mal." Politicians were winning elections by exploiting the notion of law and order and perverting definitions of safety, media outlets were supporting these ideas for their own benefit, and corporations were profiting from services to prisons and cheap prison labor. The field of prison architecture was expanding, as telephone companies were developing lucrative contracts with correctional agencies, and as the construction industry itself was thriving as a result of the many jails and prisons being built. Moreover, gender violence was increasingly conceptualized as just another crime to be addressed within the law-and-order framework by an emerging victims' rights movement supported by conservative legislators. The same condi-tions that were responsible for the economic/racial issues that drove the prison boom in the US were also responsible for ruining local economies in the Global South, and therefore driving increased migration—particularly to the US—especially from areas of the world subject to structural adjustment according to the demands of international finance capital. Immigrant detention facilities, many of them owned and operated by private prison companies, further consolidated strategies of what is now referred to as "mass incarceration." Abolition's reorientation and revitalization as a philosophical and activist tradition in the context of intensifying state violence made it possible to understand that mere reforms would not make visible or eliminate any of these structural conditions.

Because language has always been a central dimension of radical political movements, one of the explicit goals of Critical Resistance was to generate new vocabularies and new theoretical strategies that might propel scholars, artists, advocates, and organizers toward bolder critical engagements with prevailing ideologies of law and order. Two of the key terms Critical Resistance offered to the movement were "prison industrial complex" and "abolition." Both concepts were designed to eschew reformist solutions to the problem of the soaring prison population. In 1995, urban theorist Mike Davis described the California economy as moving from agribusiness toward a prison industrial complex.[17] Critical Resistance formally defined the prison industrial complex, or PIC, as "the overlapping interests of government and industry that use surveillance, policing, and imprisonment as solutions to economic, social and political problems."[18] The introduction of the concept of the prison industrial complex enabled an analysis of the prison construction boom of the 1980s and

1990s and the attendant rise in the prison population that could dispense with the naturalized assumption that those who were in prison were there simply because they had committed crimes. Based on the recognition that the use of the term *military industrial complex*, ironically introduced by then president Eisenhower as he was leaving office, helped to boost the antiwar movement during the Vietnam era, it was hoped that the related term *prison industrial complex* might also indicate a deeper analysis of the relationship between prison expansion and the political economy of racial capitalism.[19]

During this formative period of resistance, abolitionist organizers insisted on a geopolitically capacious understanding of the prison industrial complex, which, in many ways, reflected a complex feminist engagement with the relations that constitute the PIC. The preponderantly male populations of jails and prisons did not give license to dismiss gender as an important analytical category. Moreover, precisely because the PIC was conceptualized as a set of relations beyond the process of incarceration—economic, political, legal, social—it propelled activists and researchers to recognize the educational system as well as child and family services and other social service systems as domains of deeply gendered, ableist, and racialized punishment. With respect to incarceration, focusing on women's experiences of punishment also eventually helped clarify the relationships between state violence and intimate violence and to elucidate how prisons reproduce forms of violence that proliferate in the "free world."

In insisting on feminist approaches to understanding imprisonment, Critical Resistance conference organizers built on the work of coalitions of incarcerated and formerly incarcerated women to undo the notion that women were less subject to state violence because of their relatively small numbers behind bars and thus could be ignored in our efforts to understand the nature of the prison crisis. Even though women constituted a minority of people behind bars, they clearly bore the burden of criminalization and imprisonment: women have always been the major supporters of those in prison not only as organizers, but also as anchors of families and kinship networks deeply affected by incarceration practices. This is especially true of women of color. These feminist insights were directly incorporated into the structure of the 1998 Critical Resistance conference. The organizing committee spent many hours deliberating on the ways in which feminist methodologies could enhance various analyses and organizing approaches. The visible leadership of feminist activists and scholars, both in planning the conference and during the event itself, signaled that a powerful abolitionist framework required an antiracist, anticapitalist feminist practice.

Related to this insistence on feminist analytical visibility and organizing methods was the imperative to vigorously challenge ideological assumptions that often accompany and seriously pollute anti-prison work and other organizing efforts that take up existing forms of oppression—from civil rights to farmworker struggles. Entering such work has frequently entailed the implicit creation of hierarchical relations that objectify the people for whom one is working as in need of charitable assistance. This missionary position implicitly defines the beneficiaries as inferior and the benefactors as superior in relationships that are structured in such a way as to render egalitarian sociality impossible.[20] In other words, people in prison always remain "inmates" or "prisoners," just as women who experience gender violence are relegated to the status of "victims" and their advocates and helpers become categorically more capable than the objects of their charity. Prison reform movements, like anti-violence groups, even the most effective ones, have been especially susceptible to the creation of such ideologically structured relationships. As a result, people in prison (including survivors of gender and state violence) are rarely acknowledged as subjects capable of understanding and transforming their own conditions. Precisely to avoid this "charity" syndrome, Critical Resistance organizers (a group that included formerly incarcerated people) insisted that people in prison be directly involved at every level, including in the program of the conference itself. This call for inclusiveness, along with other organizing principles, reflected a feminism that was not narrowly linked to gender. Formerly and currently incarcerated people were invited to participate in as many panels as possible, even as this posed technological problems, such as installing telephone lines that permitted people behind bars to make collect calls to the conference venue. Because people in prison had generated much of the knowledge that enabled the formation of this movement to abolish imprisonment, such a conference would be seriously lacking without their direct participation.

In popularizing the framework of the prison industrial complex and developing an abolitionist critique of the punishment strategies of bourgeois democracy, abolitionists have always gestured toward a very different conception of justice. The existing criminal legal system assumes that justice is retributive, or that punishment is the very essence of justice, and naturalizes the assumption that the only way balance can be re-created in the aftermath of harm is by proportional punishment. Critics of retributive justice point to the way that vengeance, not justice, seems to drive the process. Abolition urges us to move away from myopic and individualistic conceits and to focus instead on how particular cases embody and reflect broader concerns and reveal greater threats to safety and freedom than would be evident when viewed in isolation from larger social contexts. An abolitionist analysis moves beyond the literal incarceration of bodies deemed disposable to a broader set of cruel constraints that incapacitate and police whole communities.

To generate wide-ranging conversations about the prison industrial complex, abolitionists, borrowing from cultural theorist Stuart Hall, effected a "disarticulation" of crime and punishment.[21] Popular discourses on the prison most frequently assumed that punishment existed in a causal relationship to crime, as implied by the adage "Don't do the crime, if you can't do the time." Transforming public opinion regarding the reason for soaring numbers of people in prison required convincing enough people that crime was not the unqualified cause of punishment. This process of disarticulating crime and punishment created an opportunity to engage in a politics of rearticulation to counter the notion that prison was simply the appropriate sequel for the commission of crimes with the recognition that there are many reasons people end up behind bars and many needs experienced by those who are harmed.

Central to this process of rearticulation was the recognition that race, gender, class, and sexuality were more important determinants of who goes to prison than simply the commission of a crime. In fact, the current activist practice of referring to people in prison—and this is especially true of women, both cisgender and trans—as "criminalized" rather than "criminal" helps us to understand the dangerous ideological work that the prison and the criminal legal system performs. This abolitionist and feminist attention to language and power is reflected in Eddie Ellis's "Open Letter to Our Friends on the Question of Language," published in 2007:

> (W)hen we are not called mad dogs, animals, predators, offenders, and other derogatory terms, we are referred to as inmates, convicts, prisoners, and felons—all terms devoid of humanness, which identify us as "things" rather than as people. These terms are accepted as the "official" language of the media, law enforcement, prison industrial complex, and public policy agencies. *However, they are no longer acceptable for us, and we are asking people to stop using them.*
>
> In an effort to assist our transition from prison to our communities as responsible citizens and to create a more positive human image of ourselves, we are asking everyone to stop using these negative terms and to simply refer to us as **PEOPLE**. People currently or formerly incarcerated, **PEOPLE** on parole, **PEOPLE** recently released from prison, **PEOPLE** in prison, **PEOPLE** with criminal convictions, but **PEOPLE**.[22]

This need to shift the language related to people with experiences of incarceration was also discussed and formalized in 1989 when the National Network for Women in Prison held the Fourth National Roundtable on Women in Prison in the San Francisco Bay Area, but little documentation remains of this discussion and its wide-ranging impact, a problem faced by many small organizing networks. Some documentation *does* remain—posters of convenings (but often not detailed minutes), snapshots of people gathered (but rarely lengthy summaries of the debates and discussions), images of people at actions (but not recordings of the planning meetings that shaped these strategies). The grammar and the genealogy of abolition and feminism thus sometimes rely on visual fragments and artifacts, highlighting the importance of recovering moments in abolition's past that might illuminate abolition feminist futures.

Writing with history also reveals the way in which abolitionism has always unfolded within an international context.[23] Global capitalism, financial strategies associated with the World Bank and the International Monetary Fund, and neoliberal scenarios that define poverty as individual rather than social, travel around the world alongside the exportation of carceral ideologies and strategies. Organizing the conference created opportunities to connect with anti-carceral efforts in Australia, Europe, the Middle East (especially Palestine), and South America. In the aftermath, Critical Resistance activists began to cultivate connections with campaigns in Canada, Australia, the United Kingdom, and other parts of the world.

These internationalist relations offered new ways of building interventions at the intersection of feminism and abolition. In Queensland, Australia, the organization Sisters Inside, founded by Debbie Kilroy and Anne Warner in 1992, eventually began to center abolition as the most effective solution to the incarceration of aboriginal women. They shared their organizational structure, which insists on the inclusion of currently incarcerated women in

leadership, with activists outside Australia.[24] Concurrently, the
Elizabeth Fry Societies across Canada—historically a tradition-
al charitable organization supporting women impacted by the
criminal legal system—gradually adopted an abolitionist lens,
centering organizing for decarceration, under the leadership of
current Canadian senator Kim Pate.[25]

Political prisoners in Turkey—Kurdish people and their allies—began to protest the institution of US-style prisons, called
"F-type cells" there, by engaging in prolonged hunger strikes or
death fasts. Women leaders—central to this struggle—brought
a feminist analysis to the forefront of these actions. The fact that
they specifically targeted forms of incarceration developed and
promoted by the US meant that US anti-prison activists should
pay much more attention to the global dimension of the prison industrial complex. Moreover, because feminist challenges to gender violence and socialist feminist analyses are at the core of the
ongoing Kurdish struggle for democracy, there are crucial lessons
regarding abolitionist futures to be learned.[26]

Abolition, as a tradition, a philosophy, and a theory of change,
moves away from a myopic focus on the distinct institution of the
prison toward a more expansive vision of the social, political, and
economic processes that defined the context within which imprisonment came to be viewed as the legitimate hand of justice.
As a "practical organizing tool and a long-term goal," abolition is
a political vision with the goal of eliminating imprisonment, policing, and surveillance and creating lasting alternatives to punishment and imprisonment.[27] As illustrated by the history of the
prison and the police, reforms sold as "progressive" all too often

function to mask expanding mandates, logics, and budget lines. Abolitionist movements require struggles about strategy and vision: what, for example, are the "non-reformist reforms" (to use the phrase coined by Marxist theorist André Gorz and employed by Thomas Mathiesen in his *Politics of Abolition*) that make sustainable and material differences in the lives of people living under the control of oppressive systems?[28]

Despite the long historical development of an abolition feminist framework that is both revolutionary and internationalist, mainstream interpretations of this contemporary movement have often narrowly focused on negation or absence—what abolitionists aim to remove or dismantle. In a December 2020 interview, former president Barack Obama offered a familiar critique: "Snappy slogans" such as "defund the police" are damaging. He stated: "You lost a big audience the minute you say it, which makes it a lot less likely that you're actually going to get the changes you want done." What is obfuscated by this sentiment are the immense gains and ruptures offered by the language of social and political movements. As our reliance on one critical genealogy of abolition indicates, abolition has always been as much about the work that focuses on building and experimenting as it has on what must be dismantled. As Ruth Wilson Gilmore has pointed out, "Abolition is about presence, not absence. It's about building life-affirming institutions."[29]

Building has always been central, particularly for those working at the intersection of feminism and abolition. For example, as feminists recognize the pervasiveness of gender and sexual violence, the work cannot be only to defund police, as this will not address harm endemic to communities. Abolition feminism has always required a practice, an engagement—preventative community-based responses that can be implemented to both reduce the incidence of gender and sexual violence and address harm when it does happen, without calling the police. By definition, this requires revisioning, experimentation, and engagement, not simply the absence or removal of police or prisons.

Free Our Queens, made by Melanie Cervantes and the Women In Reentry Fellows at the People's Paper Co-op to raise money for the Philadelphia Community Bail Fund, 2020.

Crucial Antecedents

Abolitionist as adjective and identity in the contemporary moment draws profoundly on the nineteenth century as inspiration. Just as racial slavery was a target of abolition then, a retributive and punishment-focused criminal legal system that has always been structurally inclined toward racist violence is the focus of abolition now. Abolition has also been compared by some to the use of the term *revolution*—amorphous, shapeshifting, defined only through use. A range of activists, scholars, and public figures mobilize it to describe a wide spectrum of work, including work designed to address the era of racial mass incarceration without putting to rest the entirety of the criminal legal system. While abolition has become a twenty-first-century term defining the standpoint of many radical activists involved in global justice movements, we can learn from a close reading of its use in the nineteenth century.

Organizers at the turn of this century understood how difficult it would be to attempt to move away from a prison system that had been made to appear natural and permanent, just as putting an end to the system of transatlantic racial slavery once seemed an impossible political goal. Analogies to the abolition of racial slavery have taken root in prison abolitionist circles, even or perhaps especially in the narrower approaches to ending mass incarceration, or in studies of the social death of slavery and the civil death of imprisonment.[30] We attempt here to distinguish between a purely analogical relation between slavery and imprisonment and one that acknowledges a genealogical connection between the two institutions. It is within the context of highlighting the historical influence of the system of slavery—with its violent and racialized punishments manifested in the development of the convict lease system and the post-slavery penitentiary system of the South—that we trace the past convergences of abolition and feminism within the antislavery movement. White women, for example, developed a consciousness of their own collective predicament by comparing the institution of marriage to slavery without attending to the violences perpetuated by their own actions and inactions. Moreover, we may want to consider that the very term *feminism*, an anglicization of the French *feminisme*, has its origin within the tradition of utopianism associated with Charles Fourier, who interpreted the social condition of women as a form of slavery.[31] There are some aspects of the relationship between the antislavery and anti-prison movements and the political moments in which they occurred that have yet to be brought into a conversation that acknowledges the pitfalls and potential of feminism.

Of the many inspirations for the work of abolitionists today, one of the most important is a text that circulated widely among lay scholars and thinkers affiliated with the Black movement before it became part of the academic canon in the 1980s. W. E. B. Du Bois's *Black Reconstruction in America: An Essay Toward a History of the Part Which Black Folk Played in the Attempt to Reconstruct Democracy in America, 1860–1880* was published in 1935, a moment of social and political reckoning much like the one we are experiencing today.[32] Written when there was an opening to new possibilities in the wake of capitalist crisis, Du Bois's volume on the history of post-slavery Radical Reconstruction and its demise not only reframed the period by centralizing Black agency in the making of a new democracy but also invited his contemporary readers to observe the crushing counterrevolutionary force of the property-holding elites. He argued that enslaved persons and free Black subjects were instrumental in the abolition of slavery, that slavery was indeed the cause of the Civil War, and that Reconstruction was more than a negation of slavery (and therefore was perceived as a threat by white property holders). His analysis offers a challenge both *to* historians of the period and *for* the present in which he wrote. These arguments also forecast the following contemporary abolitionist approaches: 1) taking leadership from those who are most directly impacted, so that the work incorporates the perspectives of the system's direct targets and not simply their more comfortably situated defenders; 2) calling for dismantling institutions that are overtly causing social and civil death; 3) broadening the liberatory agenda to include apparatuses of oppression beyond those that are specifically understood to be carceral; and 4) linking contemporary abolition praxis—or theory plus action and reflection—to questions of racial capitalism.

Du Bois not only prefigured the term racial capitalism—the idea that capitalism cannot be understood outside of a relationship to power and race—but, with an internationalist lens, he also insisted that abolition was always hinged to challenging capitalism. Toward the end of *Black Reconstruction*, Du Bois reflects on damage wrought by the spread of capitalism in the aftermath of slavery, which became especially apparent with the eruption of World War I: "The world wept and still is weeping and blind with tears and blood. For there began to rise in America in 1876 a new capitalism and a new enslavement of labor."[33] The war laid bare what Du Bois described as grotesque Profits and Poverty, Plenty and Starvation, Empire and Democracy, staring at each other across World Depression. And the rebuilding, whether it comes now or a century later, will and must go back to the basic principles of Reconstruction in the United States during 1867–1876—Land, Light and Leading for slaves black, brown, yellow, and white, under a dictatorship of the proletariat.[34]

A Depression-era text infused with the vision of what Du Bois referred to as "abolition democracy," *Black Reconstruction* was conceptualized as a history of the present, and more specifically a description of the historical developments that had produced the Jim Crow era.

Despite its necessary focus on humanizing the Black subjects who abolished slavery in remaking democracy, Du Bois's work still challenges prevailing assumptions about the project and the discipline of history. The theory of history he animates relied neither on teleology—the idea that human history would inevitably lead toward social improvement—nor on theology; it suggested instead that the arc of the moral universe does not necessarily bend toward justice. Reconstructing democracy required the labor and sacrifice of many, and the study of its suppression did not simply target southern planters and those who had owned slaves but also the northern capitalists who joined with them to consolidate the property interest in whiteness.[35]

From a collective reading of *Black Reconstruction*, we are led to reexamine the post–civil rights era, an era in which the dramatic rightward turn of the prison-building period bears a relationship to the demise of Radical Reconstruction. That relationship

Poster created in 2010 by Alexander Dwinell and Sanya Hyland commemorating the 1973 Walpole Prison uprising.

has been described analogically, as a period that is something like this one, leading Rev. William Barber, for example, in 2013 to call for a Third Reconstruction that would build on the first one in the nineteenth century and the second one in the twentieth (the modern civil rights era).

Radical Reconstructions, Not Liberal Reforms

Contemporary abolition feminists are pursuing a Radical Reconstruction. Prison abolitionists and scholars have been inspired by Du Bois's revised perspective, as well as the need to move from a narrow focus on cages and armed humans to a larger emancipatory vision encompassing all aspects of society. It was partly *Black Reconstruction* that allowed us to begin to see incarceration as on a continuum with racial slavery rather than belonging to a new and separate era of freedom. It is not enough to release people from chains. Just as Du Bois challenged the notion that slavery could be expunged as a discrete institution, leaving intact existing political and economic frameworks, abolitionists today call into question the prevailing assumption that mass incarceration can be effectively addressed without analyzing the root causes of injustice and the impact of other systems of oppression, including, in the first place, global capitalism. The overarching question posed by contemporary abolitionists: What would we have to change in our existing societies in order to render them less dependent on the putative security associated with carceral approaches to justice? is a reformulation of a central question posed by Du Bois. Du Bois asked how society can be reshaped to incorporate formerly enslaved people, providing them with access to land, education, and political power. Just as former slaves needed land or economic power, education or intellectual power, and representation in government or political power, incarcerated communities will be released from the hold of carcerality only by acquiring access to economic, intellectual, and political power. This framework resonates for abolition feminists because to render prisons and policing obsolete we must also build movements demanding that society be reshaped with the goal of eliminating gender and sexual violence and their enabling of racist and heteropatriarchal structures.

Because the Thirteenth Amendment to the US Constitution condoned the enslavement of persons lawfully convicted of criminal acts, contemporary criminal legal movements persistently center an analogy: slavery on a different scale is linked to the project and regime of the prison. Analogies can be helpful. *Prison Legal News* editor Paul Wright wrote in a 1998 article entitled "Slaves of the State" that "the effect of the Thirteenth Amendment was not to abolish slavery but to limit it to those who had been convicted of a crime."[36] The idea that imprisoned persons are "slaves of the state" circulated among Black people in prison long before scholar-activists began to probe the relation between slavery and the contemporary punishment system in the United States. This notion helped to generate important movements in prisons, especially those calling for union wages and benefits for workers in prisons. This analogy continues to surface with effect: in Ava DuVernay's film *13th*, Bryan Stevenson states that there are currently more Black men in prison than there were Black men enslaved in 1850, a point also emphatically made in Michelle Alexander's *The New Jim Crow*.[37]

The revelatory value of this statistical drama notwithstanding, historical methods that are overly reliant on analogical reasoning (that something is like something else) can often be misleading.[38] Relying on analogies often erases the imperative to do analytical work that might be more effectively accomplished by establishing a genealogical relation between the institution of slavery and the institution of the prison. Robert Perkinson's *Texas Tough: The Rise of America's Prison Empire* explores the way regimes and punishments associated with slavery made their way into the post–Civil War penitentiary system in Texas (and other southern states), thus problematizing the widespread assumption that penitentiaries in Pennsylvania and New York constituted the only important paradigms in US prison history.[39]

Complicating this landscape, the terms "slavery," "modern slavery," and "abolition" are deployed in contemporary movements that argue for *increased* investments in carcerality specifically to curtail trafficking—particularly sex trafficking—and sex work. For example, one global anti–sex trafficking organization, Polaris "is named for the North Star, which people held in slavery in the United States used as a guide to navigate their way to freedom."[40] This is further convoluted, as often campaigns and legislation that purport to only eliminate sex trafficking—for example, in the US the 2018 FOSTA and SESTA laws (the Fight Online Sex Trafficking Act and the Stop Enabling Sex Traffickers Act)—are used to police and punish domestic sex work.[41] We are therefore always careful to distinguish anti-prison and anti-police abolitionism from the deployment of the concept of abolitionism to target sex workers.

Beyond the slipperiness of analogies, the power of anti-prison organizing also propelled distorted conceptions into the mainstream. Without undermining the undeniable power and influence of texts such as Alexander's *The New Jim Crow* and Ava DuVernay's *13th* (which shares Alexander's conceptualization of history), a close reading and viewing reveals that both the book and the film frame mass incarceration as a primarily US problem that emanates from the failure to comprehensively address the economic, political, and cultural consequences of the defunct system of chattel slavery inside the United States. While both Alexander and DuVernay associate themselves with current abolitionist discourses and recognize the importance of situating the analysis of the prison crisis within a global framework, those who do not share this broader vision have often interpreted both works to mean that the problem of racialized imprisonment will be solved by conventional and domestic civil rights activism—in other words, without necessarily disturbing larger, global frameworks of power such as capitalism and heteropatriarchy.

While the term "mass incarceration" played a significant role in awakening the public to the fact that the United States incarcerates more people—both absolutely and per capita— than any other country in the world, its usage as a concept in governmental circles, both progressive and conservative, has inevitably encouraged the assumption that the decarceration of specific populations is, by itself, an adequate response.[42] Similarly, the use of the category of "innocence" is often invoked as an adequate measure of determining who gets released and who "deserves" to remain in prison. Official reactions assume that the problem of mass incarceration can be addressed by simply releasing a certain number of people from prison and that the problem of gender violence can be solved by simply imprisoning individual perpetrators—especially prominent male figures. Yet the demonstrations and uprisings in the spring of 2020 with demands to defund the police demonstrated not only that many years of developing abolitionist organizing strategies were finally having a major impact but that reform pathways—for example federal legislation like the First Step Act, which opened up potential pathways for releasing a very limited number of people from the federal system—cannot even begin to address the structural character of carceral racism.

While galvanizing wider audiences, these analogies, concepts, and texts often propelled and naturalized reforms that did not disturb the conditions of structural racism responsible for the police abuse and incarceration of so many people of color. The First Step Act, as a salient example, was greeted with resounding ovations from both liberal and conservative circles when it was finally signed into US law at the end of 2018. Hailed as "the most significant criminal justice reform bill in decades," some expressed the hope that it might serve as a step forward. Granted, a few more people in federal prisons were released earlier than previously expected, but the overall impact on the incarcerated population—on people in state prisons, county and city jails, jails in Indian Country, immigrant detention facilities, military prisons, as well as in federal prisons—will be minimal. The federal prison population of 181,000 consists of less than 10 percent of the total number of people behind bars in the United States. If the 2020 occupant of the office of the president had pardoned all those incarcerated in federal prisons, it would have simply decreased the country's imprisoned population from 2.1 million to 1.9 million.[43]

Legislation such as the First Step Act and its relatively minor measures have been embraced as important solutions to the problems included under the category of mass incarceration, which is unfortunately most often interpreted in isolation from police expansion, US Immigration and Customs Enforcement (ICE) raids, the expansion of public registries, the family policing system, and other dimensions of the prison industrial complex. The rich and extensive history of abolition feminism from the late twentieth century to the present militates against simplistic approaches to issues related to prisons, police, and gender violence. It is therefore especially disheartening, although unsurprising, to abolition feminists to witness the overly simplified strategy designed to address the continuing crisis that has been named mass incarceration, and especially to consider that the most prominent mainstream approaches to gender and sexual violence rely precisely on carceral "solutions." We know that the very history of the prison system has been one of putative reforms, which have carefully safeguarded the system itself from the kind of criticism that not only might have assisted in developing new strategies for addressing harm but also recognized that it is impossible to productively address modes of punishment without deep analyses of the socioeconomic and ideological factors that structure the societies that prisons purport to serve.

As abolitionist theory and practice demand a focus on structural forces, this attention cannot come to a standstill once we point out that these structural forces are deeply embedded in the

Poster created by Jesus Barraza of Dignidad Rebelde, 2020.

prison industrial complex. What, for instance, is the relationship between the massive numbers of Black, Indigenous, and Latinx people behind bars and the system of racial capitalism more broadly? The posing of such a question warns us about the pitfalls of assuming that racism is simply a given, and, by itself, a foundational explanatory concept needing no further examination. Such a truncated analytical sequence leads, for example, to the fallacious assumptions that what is often referred to as mass incarceration driven by racism is a peculiarly US phenomenon, even as we witness similar developments under the pressure of global capitalism in countries like South Africa, Colombia, and Brazil.

A myopic focus on the institution of the prison has protected the institution itself from abolitionist criticism. But it is not enough to focus on abolition in the narrow sense. Indeed, abolitionists have come to recognize that our advocacy must identify much more than the institution itself as the site for abolition. It is simply not possible to tear down prisons but leave everything else intact, including the structural racism that links the prison to the larger society or the heteropatriarchy and transphobia that fuels gender and sexual violence. This is the abiding message that Du Bois's *Black Reconstruction in America* conveys to activist intellectuals in the twenty-first century, as prisons and policing continue to constitute the "afterlife of slavery."[44]

Strategy: Care Not Cops

Abolition also demands that we answer to communities that want meaningful, affirming, and accessible services, including health care and housing, but not when these are annexed to punishment. Across the globe, abolitionist analysis and language emerged in a range of struggles in the second decade of the twenty-first century. Abolitionist campaigns against new jails or other forms of carceral expansion and criminal legal reform intersect with the material consequences of the state's abandonment of people with diverse needs. Delinking health care and mental health services—and so many other necessary flourishing life functions such as housing and education—from jailing and other facets of the carceral apparatus is crucial. This process of delinking represents an important principle of abolition, which is to challenge the migration of carcerality from brick-and-mortar jails and prisons to the places in everyday life where surveillance and punitive control dominate other aspects of the state's enterprise. Again, unsurprisingly, this careful work toward abolition—to parse punishment from authentic forms of care, to push back on how the state absorbs the language of community-based demands for affirmation and support and deftly translates these into coercion and repression—has always been the labor of feminists who oppose racial capitalism. As contemporary struggles around carceral expansion increasingly morph into fights about services, including health care and housing, abolition feminism guides us to organize boldly and carefully. How struggle unfolds matters.

Directly linking jails and other carceral institutions to care and treatment widens the net of the carceral state. While some might identify incarceration as the first or only place they were able to find access to health care, this should neither be praised nor become policy. As many scholars and activists suggest, drug treatment programs and mental health services, particularly in an environment where most poor people do not have access to these resources untethered to punishment, are rarely liberatory or affirming. Kerwin Kaye's research on one reform often depicted as progressive—drug courts, or courts that offer supervised treatment as an alternative to prison sentences for some drug-related crimes—illustrates that not only do approximately 50 percent of people diverted to these courts "fail" in their treatment but in order to first participate, a person must plead guilty.[45] The 50 percent who "fail" must then serve the sentence attached to their original guilty plea, and they are unable to negotiate any plea arrangements. Far from "care" or treatment, Kaye illustrates that drug courts and mandated treatment programs are simply fresh forms of "therapeutic governance," or new annexes to the prison industrial complex. Of course, unarticulated is that this "failure" does not trigger the program's or the treatment provider's accountability.

This fluid ability of the prison industrial complex to incorporate community demands for "care" and "treatment" is not novel. Disability organizers, addicts, youth activists, and particularly feminists have all recognized how vulnerability, in the form of needed care, protection, treatment, and a respect for difference, is weaponized by the carceral system.

Abolition as a forward-looking alternative to the conservative strategy of recurring yet ineffectual reforms has been enriched and deepened by theories and practices associated with the disability movement. Just as the stigma of criminalization had to be seriously challenged to persuade people that struggles against incarceration constituted worthwhile social justice activism, so the disability rights movement has had to challenge the stigma of pathologization and likewise demonstrate that disability rights are essential to human rights, and thus occupy a central place on social justice agendas. While disability activists have long argued that disability itself is a social construct and have successfully protested the institutionalization of physically, psychiatrically, and intellectually disabled people, contemporary disability studies scholars have sought to link the struggle for prison abolition with deinstitutionalization.

In the most recent work of scholar-activist Liat Ben-Moshe, *Decarcerating Disability,* she observes that "disability and madness are largely missing from analyses of incarceration and its resistance" and compellingly argues that prison abolitionists have a great deal to learn from the experience of deinstitutionalization. Challenging the prevalent assumption that deinstitutionalization of the public asylums helped to drive homelessness and the rise in incarceration, she writes:

> deinstitutionalization did not lead to homelessness and increased incarceration. Racism and neoliberalism did, via privatization, budget cuts in all service/welfare sectors, and little to no funding for affordable and accessible housing and social services, while the budgets for corrections, policing, and punishment (of mostly poor people of color) skyrocketed.[46]

Abolition feminism explicitly rejects state attempts to mobilize vulnerability and difference for the purpose of expanding carcerality and instead works to highlight the role of the state in perpetuating violence, demanding engagements that both support

Reformist reforms vs. abolitionist steps to end IMPRISONMENT

This poster is a tool to assess and understand differences between reforms that strengthen imprisonment and abolitionist steps that reduce its overall impact and grow other possibilities for wellbeing. As we work to dismantle incarceration in all its forms, we must resist common reforms that create or expand cages anywhere, including under the guise of "addressing needs" or as "updated" replacements. Jails and prisons deprive communities of resources like medical and mental health care, transportation, food, and housing. In our fights, it is critical to uplift and strategically contribute to movements led by imprisoned people, both to address pressing conditions and for abolition. In all decarceration strategies, we must utilize tactics that will improve life for those most affected and make space to build the worlds we need.

DOES THIS...	reduce the number of people imprisoned, under surveillance, or under other forms of state control?	reduce the reach of jails, prisons, and surveillance in our everyday lives?	create resources and infrastructures that are steady, preventative, and accessible without police and prison guard contact?	strengthen capacities to prevent or address harm and create processes for community accountability?

[Top table — "Reformist reforms"; each cell begins with NO.]

[Bottom table — "Abolitionist steps"; each cell begins with YES.]

DOES THIS...	reduces the number of people imprisoned, under surveillance, or under other forms of state control?	reduce the reach of jails, prisons, and surveillance in our everyday lives?	create resources and infrastructures that are steady, preventative, and accessible without police and prison guard contact?	strengthen capacities to prevent or address harm and create processes for community accountability?

A poster designed by Shana Agid for Critical Resistance in 2018 to analyze differences among reforms (see appendices for full text).

people who are most affected and address the root causes of incarceration—poverty, white supremacy, misogyny.

The absorption of "care" under the umbrella of criminalization and the blurring of the categories of social need, illness, and criminality—therapeutic governance—is achieved through the guileful mobilization of the false division between private and public spheres. Feminists have long tracked these manipulations: the state frames childcare as a private responsibility but defines fetuses, reproduction, and select caregivers/parents as a public concern subject to partisan political manipulation. For some, (hetero)sexuality is considered a private matter, but queer, HIV-positive, disabled people, and people involved in sex work are subject to state repression. Imbued with a stamp of permanence and inevitability, public/private distinctions not only engineer vulnerability—in-home support, for example, for people with disabilities is a personal responsibility that sometimes engenders risk and precarity—but race, gender, wealth, sexuality, and ability have also always defined who has access to any right to privacy. For example, some states mandate drug testing for recipients of Temporary Assistance for Needy Families (TANF) or other social assistance programs. And the public sphere is always redlined: Women—overwhelmingly non-white—who commit the "crime" of "falsely" enrolling their children in more affluent public school districts where they do not reside are charged and sentenced. In 2011 two Black mothers, Kelley Williams-Bolar and Tanya McDowell, were convicted of felonies for the "falsification of records and theft of public education" and "boundary hopping."[47] Far from neutral and static, the malleable contours of public and private not only deepen inequalities but frequently mask the evidentiary traces of racialized, ableist, and heterogendered violence.

Learning from campaigns against new proposed jails in other locations and building on decades of abolition feminist community organizing that rejected policing and incarceration as public health or safety solutions, in 2019 a Los Angeles coalition of organizations including Dignity and Power Now and Critical Resistance, defeated, for now, the proposed four-thousand-bed jail-like "treatment center" that clearly was not, as advertised, a "care-first" facility. LA had proposed this new "mental health facility" as a replacement for the crumbling Men's Central Jail and awarded a $2.2 billion dollar contract to a for-profit corporation with a track record of building jails, McCarthy Building Companies. Under the labor and leadership of community members with direct experiences of incarceration, mainly women of color, the campaign focused on educating communities that it was possible and necessary to disentangle health care services from punishment and highlighted how this could be done. The campaign also worked to make visible why the contract with McCarthy Building Companies was simply an expansion of the existing jail. As Hilda Solia, one of the members of the LA County Board of Supervisors who reversed her vote and rescinded the contract, stated, "A jail is a jail is a jail. It is not enough to change the name of the facility."[48] This is the impact of the slow work of abolition feminism in always urgent times, the slow work that has its gaze on the long term.

Another example of how the state manipulates reform agendas is electronic monitoring, which is also increasingly proposed as a kinder compromise when communities push back on new jail

or prison construction. Sometimes advanced as a progressive reform, including by some who identify as feminists, e-carceration
is lauded as not only cheaper but more humane, as it potentially
addresses the criticisms of toxic jail conditions, including lengthy
waits for trials and exorbitant bail bonds. Strategically obscured
are the high fees that people must pay for their own surveillance
devices and the rapidly expanding market for e-carceration. The
for-profit GEO Group, which operates the largest number of private prisons in the US, also controlled, under its "GEO Care" division in 2018, about 30 percent of all monitoring devices. These
forms of what James Kilgore has called "carceral humanism"
or what other scholars have termed "enlightened coercion" or
"carceral feminism," do not eliminate cages.[49] Rather they redraw
them, and thus often make them less transparent, while also widening the boundaries of policing, punishment, and surveillance
as astutely demonstrated by Victoria Law and Maya Schenwar
in *Prison by Any Other Name: The Harmful Consequences of Popular Reforms*. It is also, unsurprisingly, a deeply gendered turn:
the shift toward electronic monitoring additionally transforms
homes into prisons, and wives, mothers, granddaughters, daughters, aunties, and sisters into unpaid jailers. Even when we think
we "win" or defeat proposed jail expansion or new construction
projects, how and why and with what tools we struggle, matters.

Struggle: Reform or Abolition

Lives are at the core of every abolitionist struggle. In 2015, twenty-
two-year-old Kalief Browder (a little brother and a son whose moth-

er nicknamed him Peanut) died by suicide after being imprisoned for over two years at Rikers Island while awaiting trial for allegedly stealing a backpack. Kalief Browder was held in part because he could not post the $3,000 bail bond. Kalief Browder's death and the accompanying media attention placed both the jail and the bail bond industry under increased public scrutiny. While brown, Black, queer, and poor communities have long railed against the toxic conditions in jails and the extortion of money bonds, and while groups across New York, including the Sylvia Rivera Law Project and the New York chapters of Critical Resistance, have histories of organizing that include explicit demands for the closure of Rikers Island, Kalief Browder's death deepened mobilizations. Almost fifty years after people inside the House of D. established bail bond funds, the movement to end cash money bond, and the Campaign to Close Rikers, gained powerful momentum.

In response to mounting pressure from grassroots movements, led and shaped by abolition feminist organizing after Kalief Browder's death, in 2019 a commission appointed by then mayor Bill de Blasio proposed to close Rikers Island Correctional Facility, the largest jail in the United States, and to open new four jails, one in each borough of the city, with an estimated price tag of almost $11 billion. This plan would build what an architecture news source described in an unironic statement that borrowed from Michel Foucault's framework as "a dispersed carceral archipelago."[50]

Many recognized that four new jails would clearly expand, not shrink, the footprint of incarceration in the city of New York. The siphoning of public dollars to for-profit corporations to build carceral sites, a form of what Jackie Wang terms "racialized accumulation by dispossession," is just one of the ways that the state funnels public dollars to private coffers.[51] The majority of the $11 billion initially earmarked will go to for-profit corporations and yet payments will not stop after these jails are built. While many have rightly criticized how political and social movements against "mass incarceration" have often stalled around a narrow focus on divestment from private prisons (as if public prisons might be just fine), abolitionists contend that the ongoing dexterity of racial capitalism requires continual interrogation, particularly of how democratic forms of governance are weaponized to extract wealth from communities.

With strategic and visible direct action, creative memes and media, and organized pressure on key policy makers, No New Jails NYC (NNJNYC) coalesced and amplified resistance and offered tangible public safety strategies. That is, the NNJNYC campaign is not simply about what communities do not want, but, in the tradition of abolition feminism, is centered instead on what people need and want to be safe. Indeed, while the campaign slogan is "no new jails," the more central demand is to invest public resources into what communities recognize as support for efforts to reduce interpersonal harm and to engender safety. Community forums, workshops, and political education materials, for example, surfaced desires for a non-carceral budget that reflected serious community investment. The NNJNYC website demands "$11 Billion for the People":

> We call on the city to fund programs that actually keep us safe, reduce interpersonal conflict, and prevent our loved ones from

going to jail. These programs include: housing for all, repairing NYCHA [New York City Housing Authority] and shelter conditions; expanding comprehensive community-based and culturally responsive mental health resources; funding harm reduction programs; expanding access to education especially for people who have experienced incarceration; alleviating extreme poverty; ending mass surveillance and the extraction of wealth from communities through criminal court fines, fees, surcharges, and bail; and stopping false and illegal arrests.[52]

NNJNYC is against the construction of new jails, but more critically it provides spaces for people to grapple, together, with definitions of authentic public safety—what would make our community safer?—and subsequently generates and circulates tangible pathways. Key partners in the NNJNYC campaign are organizations, including Survived & Punished, Black & Pink, and the Audre Lorde Project, that have spent more than a decade organizing to end gender and sexual violence without relying on carceral responses. This is abolition feminism in practice.

New York City is actively advancing the plan to build four new jails to replace the buildings on Rikers Island. Yet through abolition feminist lenses and metrics—an accounting that extends beyond this immediate political moment—the wins are tangible. Political education materials circulated extensively, highlighting how public safety could be achieved by investing in communities rather than jail expansion. An array of organizations signed on to NNJNYC and made linkages connecting their work around housing justice, quality and free public transit, for meaningful and affirming health care, and against deportations and interpersonal violence. People directly impacted by policing and imprisonment and their loved ones were at the center of the organizing and analysis. Anti-violence organizations played key and visible roles, pushing back on carcerality as the solution to gender and sexual violence. The power of privately hoarded wealth and organized philanthropy to engage in carceral statecraft was temporarily rendered transparent and challenged.[53] The carceral roots of liberal Democrats received some exposure. All the tentacles related to jail expansion—including policing— were made visible and were resisted. This campaign moved the starting line for the next step in mobilization: action. The cost? The life of Kalief Browder and too many others.

II.

Feminism.

In the summer of 2020, a small group of evolving abolition feminists wrote a powerful open letter to the anti-violence movement called "The Moment of Truth."[1] Acknowledging how mainstream anti-violence interventions had relied too much on the criminal legal system and, as such, "repeatedly failed Black, Indigenous, and people of color (BIPOC) survivors, leaders, organizations, and movements," forty-seven established anti-violence coalitions from twenty states across the US signed the letter. In doing so, they demonstrated their willingness to stand in solidarity with activists who wrote that "turning away is no longer an option. Superficial reform is not enough." Indeed, the letter built on the assertion that feminist goals are not possible without abolition:

- We have failed to listen to Black feminist liberationists and other colleagues of color in the movement who cautioned us against the consequences of choosing increased policing, prosecution, and imprisonment as the primary solution to gender-based violence.
- We have promoted false solutions of reforming systems that

are designed to control people, rather than real community-based solutions that support healing and liberation.

- We have invested significantly in the criminal legal system, despite knowing that the vast majority of survivors
  choose not to engage with it and that those who do are often re-traumatized by it.

- We have held up calls for "victim safety" to justify imprisonment and ignored the fact that prisons hold some of
  the densest per-capita populations of trauma survivors in
  the world.

- We have ignored and dismissed transformative justice approaches to healing, accountability, and repair, approaches created by BIPOC leaders and used successfully in
  BIPOC communities.

Explicitly calling for the centering of leadership from Black
and Indigenous communities, as well as from other communities of color, and divestment from the criminal legal system, the
letter signified triumph and trouble. Some of the signatories—
especially those from domestic violence and sexual assault coalitions representing large numbers of very mainstream shelters and
rape crisis centers in more conservative states—faced immediate
backlash. Calling the statement "offensive" and "dangerous," the
Idaho Prosecuting Attorneys' Association, the Idaho Sheriffs'
Association, and the Idaho Chiefs of Police Association with-
drew their support for the Idaho Coalition Against Domestic and
Sexual Violence.[2] Funders called into question the focus of their
work, legislators pushed back against the analysis of how laws
have interfered with safety, police chiefs objected to being iden-

tified as part of the problem, and local service partners distanced themselves because they feared a loss of status if they identified with the brave coalition members who dared to speak out about the carceral orientation of those feminist anti-violence activists standing in the path of emancipatory strategies that would require taking abolition seriously.

At the same time, the Moment of Truth statement galvanized more general support for racial justice from anti-violence programs. It inspired Embrace, a medium-sized advocacy agency in Barron County, Wisconsin, which serves people who have been hurt by domestic violence, to write a public statement:

> In the midst of a national uprising and dialogue on state violence, Embrace adds their voices affirming the humanity and dignity of Black, Indigenous, People of Color (BIPOC). We share the global grief over the lives of George Floyd, Breonna Taylor, and Ahmaud Arbery as well as the shootings of Jacob Blake, and the many other acts of racist violence perpetrated against Black people over the past 400 years in this country. Like Martin Luther King, Jr. and Emmett Till, they will not be forgotten.
>
> As an anti-violence organization, Embrace cannot end one form of violence without addressing the other, and we cannot properly serve all survivors if we do not acknowledge and address the oppression and violence the most marginalized survivors are experiencing.[3]

This statement, like the one by Moment of Truth, argues that the root causes of racism, police violence, sexual violence, and gender-based violence are the same and that the work to end gender violence must include attention to how structural oppression and state violence shape and indeed deepen the impact on survivors and others. The statement ended with a resounding declaration: "Embrace supports the movement for Black Lives. We hear their words, lift up their voices, and stand in the anti-violence values of our organization. We hope you will join us in breaking the cycle of trauma created by racism and violence." Embrace solidified its commitment by posting a Black Lives Matter sign in the organization's front window near the prominently displayed rainbow flag signaling the organization's commitment to queer solidarity.

As individual programs and statewide anti-violence coalitions expressed support for Black Lives Matter and pulled back from engagement with the carceral state, police departments, prosecutors, state attorneys, and other entities immediately began to sever ties with these anti-violence programs. Embrace's powerful words and impassioned invitations were met with immediate disdain from key community leaders. The Barron County Board of Supervisors halted funding to the organization, reducing its budget by $25,000. Along with four area police departments, the Barron County Sheriff's Department cut ties with the agency, which likely means they will no longer refer people who need assistance to Embrace for emergency services. Other anti-violence groups that have taken vocal positions like Embrace and the signatories of the Moment of Truth statement have experienced similar forms of swift retaliation from law enforcement and other state and carceral entities.[4] The speed with which relationships between carceral actors and anti–gender violence groups with abolitionist orientations unraveled reveals their inherent fragility.

The organizing work that produced the Moment of Truth statement—and the backlash that resurfaced decades-old tensions between feminist work against gender violence and abolitionist demands to close prisons—was reminiscent of earlier conflicts between activists focusing on racist state violence and those calling for an end to domestic violence. A political misalignment that had been simmering just below the surface was, once again, on display. Carceral policy makers, law enforcement organizations, conservative funders, mainstream service providers, and many academic researchers were, for the most part, unwilling to acknowledge that programs targeting gender violence should be concerned with advancing racial justice and were reluctant to consider that survivors of gender violence might be harmed, rather than helped, by police. One of the most pointed examples of this tension was the lead story in the widely circulated *Domestic Violence Report* ("Another Perspective on 'The Moment of Truth Statement'"), which criticized abolitionist demands and claimed that "survivors do not support defunding the police."[5] The report's broad claims about the role of policing in creating safety for those who experience gender violence blatantly ignores what many women and nonbinary people of color have been asserting for years: because systemic racism drives the criminal legal system, it is not only not protective for those survivors who are not part of the mainstream, it also endangers them.

Indeed, tensions between abolition and feminism, exemplified by the article in *Domestic Violence Report*, are as old as they are familiar. Precisely at the moment domestic violence and sexual assault were being recognized as crimes, thus presumably requiring carceral responses, contemporary abolitionists were effectively challenging a criminal legal system that naturalized retributive punishment. Unfortunately, the abolition work that emerged in the early 1970s did not necessarily attend to questions of gender violence despite the presence of feminist leadership. For some leaders in both movements, this discord, both philosophical and political in nature, was treated as a fundamental roadblock. For others, decades of work in this movement illustrated this stark reality: while it is critical to hold those who use violence accountable, advocating for greater involvement by the criminal legal system is counterproductive at best, and can actually further endanger some survivors.[6]

The analysis of abolition feminism that we advance in this book is predicated on the indivisibility of abolition and feminism. Abolition is stronger and more effective precisely because of its feminism. On the other hand, gender justice will not be realized without the incorporation of abolition praxis. Beyond the challenges posed by adversary forces, abolition feminists recognize the necessary intersection of questions raised both by anti-violence activists and abolitionists. For example, do calls for defunding the police fully reckon with the danger of having classified gender violence as a crime like any other leading to even larger investments in police and prisons? Or do analyses of the way structural racism in the criminal legal system promotes transphobia also include attention to disability justice? Where is the feminist imperative to acknowledge intersectionalities of struggles—as an explicit politics and praxis—in current abolitionist mobilizations? Where is the sustained political commitment to abolition in feminist anti-violence work? These are urgent questions, posed here as part of a rhetorical strategy for rethinking the current movement and to invite a recognition within the more prominent genealogy of abolition of its roots in radical organizing against both state and intimate violence. We return here to the historical legacies of abolition feminism as a way of showing how women of color and other radical anti-violence activists have long called for divestment from the criminal legal system.

Illustration by Cristy C. Road, 2003, featured on the cover of the INCITE! toolkit, *Law Enforcement Violence Against Women of Color & Trans People of Color*, published in 2018.

INCITE!

The abolition feminism at work in the Moment of Truth statement emerged as a consequence of long-term and persistent organizing, coupled with deep thinking about that work, represented by the histories with which this book engages. Here, we offer snapshots from one particular origin story, the founding of INCITE! Women of Color Against Violence (later Women, Gender Non-Conforming, and Trans People of Color Against Violence). While INCITE! was not alone in pioneering new, intersectional analyses, we believe it played a critical role as it attempted to interrupt the political effects of criminalization and as it strongly reprimanded those feminisms that raced to embrace carceral solutions.

For INCITE! the call for change came primarily from women of color activists in the late 1990s who firmly insisted that after thirty years of trying to reform anti-violence organizations from the inside, it was time to turn to more radical work. Women of color activists who had dedicated our lives to working against the tyranny of gender violence and for justice for our communities found ourselves struggling for years to remake organizations that offered simplistic, neoliberal responses to complex problems. These groups unquestionably assigned blame to individual perpetrators of violence rather than looking more deeply into oppressive social structures, whose culpability is ideologically foreclosed. This more radical work was necessary because by the late 1990s a social justice–oriented anti-violence movement had been effectively coopted by the state, and anti-violence programs had been transformed from a network of radical, grassroots self-help groups into a highly professionalized service-based industry.

In 2000, a small group of eighteen women of color anti-violence organizers decided to finally and absolutely reject the reformist project of trying to hold dominant anti-violence organizations accountable for their complicity with and reliance on the carceral state.[7] This group had gathered for the purpose of honing an analysis of gender violence that accentuated its relation to state violence, especially within the context of racism. Determined to contest existing leadership paradigms, they decided unapologetically to refuse compromises that marginalized race, class, sexuality, immigration status, or disability as secondary issues. In the very process of this deliberate organizing and collective theorizing, they were embarking on a path that transformed political fatigue and frustration into joyful revolutionary rage. As was later the case for the Moment of Truth statement, the call was not only to *critique* what was wrong or inadequate, but also—and even more importantly—to *build* the larger liberation movement without which we would never end gender violence. Anti-violence organizations—like the Coalition Against Rape and Abuse (CARA), Sista II Sista, the Audre Lorde Project, and INCITE!—embraced this analysis, developing and practicing on-the-ground responses to gender and sexual violence, often explicitly identifying as abolition feminist formations.

Like Critical Resistance, INCITE! began in a convening in the year 2000 that reflected a hunger for radical ideas and practices. The conference, "The Color of Violence: Violence Against

Women of Color," was organized with a number of goals. First, the conference planners hoped to provide an opportunity for women of color activists to revise and deepen radical analyses and corresponding strategies around ending gender violence by centering antiracist and anti-imperialist struggles. The vision was less about emphasizing how the work had become more conservative and more about reclaiming the political power that characterized early women-of-color-led activism around gender violence. It was an attempt to reverse the fact that "[w]e won the mainstream but lost the movement."[8] Second, conference organizers hoped to revoke the tendency to consider gender violence in isolation from other forms of violence. Moving beyond merely responding to partner violence and sexual assault, this more expansive approach led to the inclusion of immigrant rights, Indigenous treaty rights, and reproductive justice, as well as the violence of incarceration and militarism. This more inclusive analysis also identified the profound and persistent harm of homophobia and heterosexism within mainstream movement work. Shaped by abolitionist organizing and feminist analysis, INCITE! advanced the idea that gender violence was systemic and symptomatic of larger patterns of oppression. Importantly, the conference agenda encouraged practical involvement in political organizing campaigns and centrally, a transition from providing highly regulated emergency crisis intervention services and toward advancing social justice strategies to ensure safety.

These goals, with an implicit focus on what we might now call abolition feminism, grew out of the concern that the once-radical analysis of gender violence had become so mainstream that essential elements of the movement had been erased. For example, the legacy of Black lesbians and the contributions of other feminists of color who had simultaneously worked within community-based racial justice groups *and* within predominantly white feminist organizations was entirely excluded from the dominant collective movement memory. In a righteous celebratory atmosphere, the Color of Violence conference recentered the radical antiracist work that activated the movement to end gender violence in the first place.[9]

The mere *idea* of the Color of Violence conference ignited an infectious energy. This enthusiasm made it clear that women of color had yearned for years for such a space and were ready to propel the work forward based on the mandates of abolition feminism. Women of color across the country and from beyond US borders went to great lengths to attend, including pooling scarce resources, arranging for coverage at home, and driving for days to reach California. Originally planned for two hundred participants, the first Color of Violence conference ultimately drew one thousand people. Another thousand people who wanted to attend were turned away for lack of space. To address the historical legacy of racism within the anti-violence movement, strong measures were taken to ensure that this time, the conversations would proceed differently. The conference allowed only a small number to attend who were not women of color; others who participated were required to sponsor attendance for women of color, encouraged not to dominate the main sessions, and instructed not to participate in the strategy sessions unless specifically invited to do so. This was more than a series of symbolic gestures. It solidified the insistence that the work of INCITE! would not be concerned with negotiation, appeasement, or even with challenging mainstream

Dandelions & Butterflies by art twink made in collaboration with Jennicet Gutiérrez and Forward Together for Trans Day of Resilience, 2018.

anti-violence activists about their failures. Instead, the work was about strategically and enthusiastically advancing an antiracist, anticapitalist analysis of gender violence and re-centering social justice and freedom.

Since then, and for over twenty years, grassroots chapters and affiliates of INCITE! across the United States have organized broad-based social justice campaigns to link gender violence to other forms of harm. INCITE! has always been a voluntary collective, without paid staff except for episodic and discrete tasks associated with planning conferences, producing political education materials, or developing social media campaigns. In New Orleans, for example, the chapter supported low-income and uninsured women of color after Hurricane Katrina, demonstrating again how they were the ones pushing for the survival of their communities when government and nonprofit responses continued to perpetuate abusive and harmful practices. The Philadelphia chapter organized around housing and gentrification, while Brooklyn's INCITE! affiliate, Sista II Sista, worked against the sexual harassment of women of color by the New York City Police Department.

The national INCITE! collective has organized conferences and movement events, including "Building a Movement" (2002) in Chicago, "Stopping the War on Women of Color" (2005) in New Orleans, "The Revolution Will Not Be Funded: Beyond the Non-Profit Industrial Complex" (2004) in Santa Barbara, California, and "Beyond the State: Inciting Radical Possibilities" (2015) in Chicago. In order to share political analyses and to archive this radical work, INCITE! published two anthologies. *Color of Violence: The INCITE! Anthology* (2006) included writings from thirty-three radical feminists of color, with a sharp focus on federal Indian law, adoption policy, reproductive justice, Palestinian resistance, and law enforcement. Four years after the 2004 conference, INCITE! published *The Revolution Will Not Be Funded: Beyond the Non-Profit Industrial Complex*, which explored the impact of the nonprofit system on revolutionary movement building. Circulating globally, these forms of political education, like the "Community Accountability Toolkit" and the "Anti-Militarism Toolkit," have deepened the project of abolition feminism and in turn reshaped contemporary anti-violence work.

These feminist abolitionist communities came together out of a sense of desperation and from a place of love and honor that in later years proved to be much more complicated. But a sense of frustration and feelings of betrayal from abandoned commitments of solidarity from collaborators did not dissuade the organizers who continued to do the work. Those who had initially responded to the INCITE! call brought energy, hope, and the conviction that a different way was possible. This optimism—which brought a sense of urgency, and belief in the possibility of anti-violence work that resonated more broadly—was infectious and quickly spread across the country and beyond US borders. At the same time, this overarching optimism managed to overshadow important disagreements and enduring controversies. Formalized local chapters, loose affiliates, and countless individuals considered themselves members of INCITE! Engaging in small and large resistance projects—protesting new prisons, providing mutual aid, collective reading and writing for political education campaigns, and most importantly supporting survivors of gender violence in all its varied forms—INCITE! also confronted harm within its own ranks and struggled with internecine tensions and betrayals. Among the most serious failures over the twenty-year history of INCITE! was the initial exclusion of trans people in the framing of the work. It is now virtually axiomatic that any effective challenge to gender violence must center the multiple violences inflicted on trans and gender nonconforming people. Like many networks, INCITE! struggled to establish systems of accountability and transparency. More recently, widely publicized investigations regarding Indigenous identities of founding members have come to light. These are critical aspects of INCITE!'s history and must be factored into any story of its achievements. In exploring genealogies of abolition feminism, it should be pointed out that INCITE!'s influence *as a movement and a political identity* embodying a radical abolition feminism went far beyond its influence as an organization. Even as it struggled, sometimes unsuccessfully, with an array of organizational problems, the enduring legacy of INCITE!'s anticapitalist, antiracist internationalism, is what drives abolition feminism. An ongoing challenge to carceral feminism, it is a collective commitment to end all forms of violence—from the bedroom to the streets to police stations and prison cells. It is a collective commitment to forge new futures grounded not in violence but in the flourishing of life.

Radical Beginnings, Again

We situate INCITE! within a genealogy of abolition feminism because it signals how radical feminists of color have historically troubled gender essentialism, forging over time a collective political consciousness of gender violence as always also shaped by racism, class bias, transphobia, heterosexism, and so on. This genealogy resists mainstream histories of anti-violence movements that continue to center whiteness and carceral responses. While it is true that a major catalyst for the late 1960s women's movement was the recognition of the ubiquity of physical and sexual abuse of women within circles that had previously demanded their silence, there is a long history of work against sexual abuse and gender violence more broadly linked to what we now recognize as Black feminist activism. The fact that the US anti-violence movement is often conventionally periodized in connection with the 1966 founding of the National Organization for Women (NOW) and the later creation of a NOW task force on rape, erases signal contributions of women of color. While gender violence has always crossed borders of race and class, the speakouts and consciousness-raising sessions (the strategy of encouraging women to publicly reveal violence within intimate relationships that they had previously kept secret) that attempted to break the silence regarding rape and domestic violence were primarily associated with white feminism. To be sure, these teach-ins, speakouts, and consciousness-raising sessions were radical political acts. But women of color, white working-class women, and others with a more expansive political consciousness insisted on making important linkages to antiracism, reproductive justice, anti-imperialist campaigns, labor movements, and other social justice struggles. For example, radical white women activists who were part of Santa Cruz Women Against Rape released the 1977 "Letter to the Anti-Rape Movement," which stated that

Third World Women's Alliance newsletter, *Triple Jeopardy*, 1971.

letter to the anti-rape movement

This is an open letter to the anti-rape movement. We, the members of Santa Cruz Women Against Rape, are writing this letter because we are concerned about the direction the anti-rape movement is taking. While we have many concerns, some of which are expressed in this letter, we would primarily like to address the issue of the relationship of the anti-rape movement to the criminal justice system. The reasons we are interested in this issue have a lot to do with how we see ourselves as a Women Against Rape group. We are a political group that focuses on the issue of rape and violence against women, and that is working towards the long range goal of a radical transformation of the very basis of our society. We do not believe that rape can end within the present capitalist, racist, and sexist structure of our society. The fight against rape must be waged simultaneously with the fight against all other forms of oppression.

When the organized movement against rape first started about five years ago , most of the anti-rape groups were collectives of feminists, who came together because of their anger at the way the police and the courts treated rape victims.[1] These groups (and ours was among them) were primarily political. We were critics of the police, the courts, and the hospitals, the institutions that traditionally dealt with rape victims. Their awful treatment of women became a topic in the media, largely due to the efforts of the women's movement against rape. In a snowballing fashion, many other anti-rape groups formed. Many of these groups, however, did not consider themselves political, nor even feminist. They considered themselves service groups, who wanted "to help rape victims". They felt that the criminal justice system and the anti-rape movement had a common cause, "to get rapists off the street". Therefore, these groups tended to encourage or cajole women to report rapes to the police.

The more explicitly political groups were frustrated, both by the ineffectiveness and unresponsiveness of the criminal justice system, and because of the increasing rape rate. While many remained critical of the criminal justice system in theory, most groups felt it was important to work on building or improving relationships with the police and other criminal justice agencies. They hoped that this would lead to increased prosecution and conviction of rapists. In attempts by anti-rape groups to build good relations with the criminal justice system, criticism of these agencies has been withheld, or dealt with through police channels instead of by applying outside pressure (e.g. through the media, demonstrations, etc.).This tendency to work with the criminal justice system is reinforced by the fact that many groups are supported through government funds. Because of this, there is an inevitable push--if not out-right contractual obligation to persuade women to report rapes to the police.

a choice?

Many groups claim that they are neutral about reporting a rape to the police: they say they neither push a woman into it, nor tell her she shouldn't report. Their literature and phone counseling is biased toward giving women information on how to report a rape and what the police and hospital procedures are. They don't present any other options besides going to the police or doing nothing. Therefore, if a woman feels that she'd like to do something about her rape, but the only thing she is told about is the police, her probable choice would be to go to the police. Because there aren't many other alternatives, we support the right of individual rape victims to go through the criminal justice system. We don't feel that she should be forced or pushed into anything, whether reporting or not reporting a rape to the police. But as anti-rape groups, we have the responsibility to expose the function, and challenge the process, of the criminal justice system. Attempts at "good relations" with the criminal justice system have served to co-opt our movement, and have led to the belief (or hope) that the criminal justice system can solve the problem of rape. Yet, the sexist and racist nature of the criminal justice system only makes the problem worse.

We are opposed to the criminal justice system orientation o^f many anti-rape groups for a number of reasons. The criminal justice system has shown itself to be unresponsive and insensitive to the needs of women. The ordeal of reporting a rape and seeing it through trial is made painful and degrading. Even if the individuals involved try to be pleasant and helpful, the processes and structure of the system remain hostile and unsupportive to rape victims. This is largely because the women involved have no power in the process: it is the police that decide if she was "really raped", the DA often decides that it isn't a "good case" so won't prosecute, and juries hesitate to convict a rapist.

keeping the end in sight

It is true that the conviction rate for rapists is very low. This is largely due to sexism and the sexist myths about rape in our culture. We abhor the reasons for this low conviction rate but that doesn't mean that we should work for a high convictions rate. Those convicted of rape are most likely to be Third World and/or poor White men, as is true for convictions for nearly all other crimes. In order for a DA to "win" a rape case, he (or rarely, she) must use sexist, racist and classist stereotypes and assumptions, thereby supporting the worst aspects of the system. If the goal of this process is fighting and ending rape, it is bad and self defeating to use racist and classist means to get to that end. The process is crucial to the true success of the end.

The answer is not just to get rapists "off the street". Prisons themselves are incapable of changing rapists. Prison culture is much like that of the outside world, with all of the pressure intensified. Male sex roles, violence, and power relations which lead to rape in the first place, are strongly reinforced within prison. Rapists in prison don't stop raping--they simply enforce their power over men weaker than themselves. Prisons don't deal with the roots of the problem, they only add to the causes. Men getting out of prison have not learned new ways of relating to women and haven't developed an analysis of why they rape or how to change. It is likely that they will rape again.

In addition, the emphasis of many anti-rape groups on getting women to prosecute leads to a very narrow focus on a few specific rape situations. This ignores the totality of the problem. Most women experience varying degrees of violence in their everyday lives--from friends and lovers as well as from strangers. The answer to this situation is not to prosecute all cases(which is impossible and impractical as well as useless), but to work on creating more alternatives for people in their lives. This involves changing the institutions and culture which promote sexism, racism, and violence.

Those anti-rape groups who spend time working for reform legislation encounter many of the same problems and obstacles. Sexist attitudes (and actions) cannot be legislated away. Legislation does not exist in isolation; even "good" anti-rape legislation (and it isn't clear what that would be) will be ineffective in a sexist society that encourages violence against women, and in a criminal justice system that persecutes Third World and poor White men.

centering ourselves

The time and energy that is now used to develop a good working relationship with the criminal justice system agencies, and on reform legislation, could be much better spent. Instead, the anti-rape movement should work on community education, and on developing practical alternatives that deal with both the system and the roots of sexism and violence. We want our focus to be the creation of various community based and supported alternatives, because we think that the responsibility for dealing with rape should be in the hands of all community people. Some of the ideas and alternatives we're working on now include:

1. We encourage people to get together to discuss ways to watch out for each other. This includes block watching to make neighborhoods safe, organizing at workplaces to get support to deal with hassles from bosses and fellow workers, and organizing at schools to get self-defense classes, etc.

2. We try to create the consciousness in people that they should respond to a scream or a call for help, and that they should go to a woman's aid if it looks like she's being hassled.

3. We print the descriptions of men who rape, hassle and assault women so that rape will become a public issue, so that these men will lose their anonymity, and so women can be warned of some particular men.

4. Confrontations of rapists, etc. by women (or women and men). The message we want to present to men is that we know who they are and what they did, that they are responsible for their actions, and that they have the responsibility to change. We try to offer follow up re-education by anti-sexist men. Although we think that each individual confrontation is important, we hope that each one will have the more widespread effect of encouraging people to force men to stop violent and sexist behavior. This means that people have to deal with the men close to them--their family, friends, etc., as well as with strangers who hassle women.

Confrontations can be good for women who've been raped or hassled because they allow her to be active and powerful in a situation it is safe for her to be so. She can make the decisions about how a confrontation will take place and what she'd like to say. We can help her get together a group of women who will be supportive to her during this process. This is very different from reporting a rape to the police where the woman's role is a passive one (as a witness for the state) and where others make decisions about her case for her. (Contact us for more information about confrontations.)

continued on page 10

First page of "Letter to the Anti-Rape Movement" by Santa Cruz Women Against Rape, published by *Off Our Backs* in 1977.

the "racist and sexist" criminal legal system makes the problem of rape "worse."[10] Even the term "women of color," popularized during that era, signified the political formation of a radical feminist alliance among women who shared oppression from a range of structural forces in addition to heteropatriarchy, including the generalized criminalization of their communities.

Without underestimating the eventual emergence of a strong anti-rape and anti-violence movement, an abolition feminist lens troubles conventional histories that too frequently still center white women and mainstream organizations. The group Sisters Testify (ST) is a storytelling project dedicated to ensuring that Black women's resistance to sexual abuse is not lost in the historical accounts of anti-violence movement organizing. ST is focused on lifting up the work that Barbara Ransby, Deborah King, and Elsa Barkley Brown lead in response to the sexual harassment and legal mistreatment of Anita Hill by the soon-to-be-appointed US Supreme Court justice Clarence Thomas. African American Women in Defense of Ourselves (AAWIDO) was formed in 1991 after 1,600 Black women and our allies signed a letter that appeared in the *New York Times* expressing "The particular outrageous racist and sexist treatment of Professor Anita Hill," and that "the malicious defamation of Professor Hill insulted all women of African descent and sent a dangerous message to any woman who might contemplate a sexual harassment complaint." ST is one of many projects attempting to more fully describe the genealogy of abolition feminism by keeping the story of AAWIDO alive. These erasures continue: Alyssa Milano, a white actor, was initially credited with the creation of #MeToo to emphasize the pandemic dimensions of sexual violence in 2017 even though Black feminist Tarana Burke had first used #MeToo in 2006. Many contemporary images associated with #MeToo, Time's Up, and campus-based Title IX initiatives are still overwhelmingly white, reflecting the institutionalized responses to sexual violence that are aligned with carceral feminism.

In this context we might ask why the important work against rape and sexual violence within the US southern Black freedom movement was so marginalized that only after many years of research and activism did we come to recognize, for example, Rosa Parks as a forerunner of the anti-rape activists in the late 1960s. Rosa Parks, Esther Cooper Jackson, Anne Braden, and others linked anti-rape strategies to campaigns against the racist use of the rape charge in the cases of the Scottsboro Nine (1931–1937), Willie McGee (1945–51), and the 1955 murder of Emmett Till, who was accused of making sexual comments to a white woman. As many scholars and activists have observed, the struggle to defend Black men from fraudulent rape charges was directly linked to the defense of Black women who were targets of rape like Recy Taylor: rape and the racist manipulation of the rape charge were fundamentally connected.[11] Much of the early work of Black feminism and radical women of color feminism consisted of attempts to correct the historical record—pointing out that white women were not the only women who challenged misogyny and patriarchy and that women of color engaged these challenges in more complex, intersectional ways.

If we acknowledge the history of contemporary calls for abolition feminism raised by the Moment of Truth statement (and related activist efforts from groups like Love & Protect, API-Chi, and Just

Practice) that can be traced back to nineteenth-century attempts by abolitionists to link antislavery strategies to women's suffrage and other feminist projects, then a critical genealogy of abolition feminism cannot exclude the lineage that proceeds from the important work against gender violence linked to movements against racist repression during the McCarthy era. Because this work has been subject to erasure or misrepresentation, only recently have scholars conducted the research that has rendered visible important contributions by major forerunners of Black feminism during the 1940s and 1950s. We often begin the story of twentieth-century Black feminism (and of intersectionality as a feminist methodology) with Fran Beal's 1969 germinal pamphlet "Double Jeopardy: To Be Black and Female," which was republished in 1970 in Toni Cade Bambara's anthology *The Black Woman* and as well in Robin Morgan's 1970 edited collection *Sisterhood Is Powerful*. However, more than twenty years before "Double Jeopardy," the Trinidadian Communist Claudia Jones wrote an extended article entitled "An End to the Neglect of the Problems of the Negro Woman!" in which she argued that Black women were subject to "superexploitation."[12] Moreover, she insisted that the occupation of domestic worker to which the majority of Black women were relegated during the decades following slavery was associated with the very dangers that Black women had experienced *during* slavery: rape, sexual abuse, and harassment more broadly. Claudia Jones clearly understood the structural nature of sexual violence.

If Claudia Jones's use of the term "superexploitation" points to an implicit understanding both of racial capitalism and the impact of patriarchy, this redaction of the Marxist critique of political economy was embraced by a larger community of radical Black women activists, who also understood the implications of the primary occupation open to Black women. Esther Cooper Jackson, a leading figure in the Southern Negro Youth Congress in the 1940s and the founding editor of *Freedomways*, wrote her 1940 master's thesis on *The Negro Domestic Worker in Relation to Trade Unionism*.[13] Long before Ella Baker emerged as a leading figure in the mid-twentieth-century Black freedom movement, she was an organizer for the NAACP, and in 1935 she and Marvel Cooke wrote an article for the NAACP's magazine *The Crisis* entitled "Bronx Slave Market."[14] The gatherings of Black women on city street corners seeking work as domestics were known as "slave markets" not only because of the exceedingly low wages but also because the conditions of work were more akin to slavery than to wage labor. Despite the prevailing euphemistic descriptions of sexual abuse, all these activists were clearly aware of harassment and sexual violence as a routine hazard of the occupation. In an interview quoted in Baker and Cooke's article, one woman indicated that she left her job not only because of the drudgery of the work but also because one of the family's adult sons had so-called hand trouble. Like Esther Cooper Jackson, Baker and Cooke also emphasized the central importance of organizing domestic worker unions.

Despite the whitewashing of the history of anti-violence organizing across the decades and the tendency to ignore racism within the anti-violence movement at different points in time, women of color continued to organize against gender and sexual violence. For example, in 1980, at the first national conference on Third World Women and Violence in Washington, DC, led by early abolition feminists like Loretta Ross and Nkenge Toure, groups like San Francisco Women Against Rape, the New York Asian Women's Center, the National Black Feminist Organization, and the Women of Color Caucus of the National Coalition Against Domestic Violence were beginning to stake out their rightful place in the landscape of anti-violence organizing. These networks built on the organizing of groups like Women of All Red Nations which, in 1974, began to address a range of issues central to the lives of Indigenous women including but not limited to interpersonal violence. These organizations' actions were dynamic, political and cultural, expansive and aspirational—fundamentally abolitionist—and often centered a transnational and postcolonial feminism. Literary and arts organizations circulated the political analysis of women of color feminisms. Kitchen Table Press published key anthologies like Cherríe Moraga and Gloria Anzaldúa's *This Bridge Called My Back* and Barbara Smith's *Home Girls*. Sweet Honey in the Rock, led by one of the original Student Nonviolent Coordinating Committee (SNCC) Freedom Singers, Bernice Johnson Reagon, provided a musical background to movement organizing. The climate of this era, ripe with hope, sprinkled with joy, was foundational to the kind of organization INCITE! aspired to be—one that was not engaged in the misery of reforming dominant organizations. Instead, this example of abolition feminism at work consisted of a network of activists bound together by a vision of what the world could be and grounded in a shared history of righteous early organizing. After years of feeling disheartened and betrayed by mainstream anti-violence activism, founding members (and those now working alongside them) desired to return to these vibrant earlier moments when radical anti-violence work embraced the celebration of our relationships and accomplishments and was driven by the passion for justice. The commitment to build on that legacy—working for freedom instead of merely working against danger and despair—was an important element of abolition feminist organizing.

Within these coalitions, currently and formerly incarcerated women, many of whom were survivors of gender violence, mobilized to redefine safety and increasingly began to fight for abolition.[15] In 1985, the first public hearing on battered women and the criminal justice system was held at Bedford Hills Correctional Facility, a maximum-security women's prison in New York, where incarcerated women centered the links between criminalization and gender violence.[16] Organized by women who were incarcerated and their anti-violence advocates on the outside, the twelve testimonies firmly established gender violence as a pathway to women's imprisonment. These hearings illuminated the profound and persistent ways that gender violence, including intimate partner violence and state violence, intersected and contributed to the incarceration rates of both women and the people who hurt them. Consistently, incarcerated women (who are not named in the report for safety reasons) testified that police failed to offer solutions: "I felt that they were giving my husband consent to come back and beat me some more after they left, and he did." These testimonies led, unfortunately, to a set of recommendations in the final report that actually enhanced the criminal legal response to gender violence—more police training, harsher penalties—in part because they ignored the context of state violence. That is, while the report attempted to center the experience and analysis of criminalized survivors, its narrow analytical frame stands as an example of why abolition feminism is so important.

Centering the experience and analyses of people in prison and the linkages between state and interpersonal violence, this organizing at Bedford built on earlier work, including self-defense and freedom organizing campaigns for incarcerated women such as the 1974 Free Joan Little movement and the emergence of 1970s groups such as Aid to Incarcerated Mothers, Prison MATCH (Prison Mothers and Their Children), and other convenings such as the 1977 "Action Conference of Women Against Repression and Prison," which gathered 120 participants, most of whom were formerly incarcerated women and others who were representative of prison justice organizing.[17] This work seeded the ground for the emergence of a wide array of groups led by currently or formerly incarcerated people, including the National Network for Women in Prison; Justice Now!; Chicago Legal Advocacy for Incarcerated Mothers; the Women's Prison Association; and later the California Coalition for Women in Prison; Women on the Rise Telling Her Story; the Transgender, Gender Variant and Intersex Justice Project; and Moms United Against Violence and Incarceration. Concurrently, networks grew centering both an abolitionist framework and the experience of criminalized survivors, including Black & Pink, Survived & Punished, and the Sylvia Rivera Law Project.[18] Increasingly abolition feminist in practice and orientation, most of these survivor-led groups continue to work inside and outside of prisons and jails to center racial justice, construe carcerality broadly (including

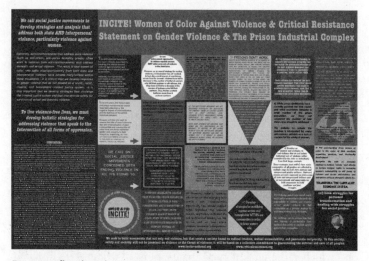

Poster reflecting the 2001 *INCITE!-Critical Resistance Statement on Gender Violence & The Prison Industrial Complex* (see appendices for full statement).

the violence inherent to social service and child welfare agencies), and challenge racial capitalism and the false solutions made available by the prison industrial complex.[19]

Carceral Cooptation and Carceral Feminism

Despite years of relentless work, by the 1990s the gulf between abolitionist perspectives and gender work was widening, and many survivors were falling into the dangerous space between the two movements. The language and analysis of radical activists was also being coopted and absorbed by mainstream organizing, as legal and legislative changes advanced local pro-arrest policies and mandatory police responses. Distracted by a false sense of success and the perception of mainstream political support, mainstream anti-violence organizations were increasingly supported by state resources, focused on data collection and service delivery models, and organized and professionalized according to a hierarchy dominated by white people. Crisis services began to mirror other neoliberal intervention programs populating the landscape of a growing social service industry. Beth Richie and Kayla Martensen later described the way in which "services became safety."[20] The emphasis of these programs was on individual care rather than root causes of violence, reforming systems rather than creating alternatives, and providing short-term respite for people who have been harmed rather than producing long-term structural changes. This cluster of organizations, from mainstream anti-violence organizations to "charities" that provide access to food or housing, are now increasingly referred to as part of a nonprofit industrial complex.[21]

Mimi Kim and other scholar-activists have documented how the self-help activities that initially characterized the anti-violence movement of the early 1970s were coopted as activists became more engaged in the work of systems advocacy and building coalitions with state actors authorized to control "crime."[22] As the work evolved and took on a more conservative tone, issues of racial injustice, sexual exploitation, pernicious state violence, and the analysis of linked forms of oppression became incompatible with an emerging conceptualization of gender violence that relied exclusively on gender essentialism.[23] Within this framework, the legitimate victim of gender and sexual violence could not be a sex worker, a queer person, a woman of color, and certainly could not be an incarcerated person. This conceptualization was predicated on false assumptions of solidarity and a uniformity of experiences of violence. More importantly, it disavowed concerns about injustice as the root of the problem, leading instead to an overly simplistic carceral analysis that promoted policing and prisons as the solution.

To its credit, this mainstream, highly visible work against gender violence firmly established that intimate relationships are sites of serious harm for women. Those with access to the developing system were provided some relief from the tyranny of abuse: over 25 percent of all cisgender heterosexual women report having been hurt by someone they are or have been in a relationship with, which could include a husband, a non-cohabitating sexual partner, or a former significant other.[24] Mainstream researchers and organizers gathered and made available this kind of data, and while this was an important and transformative accomplishment, the data were asymmetrical and incomplete: for example, larger questions about gender socialization and heteropatriarchy—the systems and communities that legitimate gender and sexual violence—and alternative responses that do not rely on the carceral state remained underexplored and therefore invisible.

The collection and dissemination of statistical data described the problem in quantitative terms, which resonated with mainstream audiences and policymakers, but did not reveal the full extent of the harm nor the root causes of gender violence. Chronic abuse from an intimate partner is profoundly worsened by its consequences: the emotional degradation, social isolation, economic dependency, and sense of shame and alienation from one's body and spirit that typically comes with physical and sexual abuse. For people who are undocumented, disabled, using illegal substances, financially insecure, queer, older, or impacted by the criminal legal system, the vulnerability to gender violence may be even more profound. People of color, those without secure housing, women who are responsible for care for others, and young queer people who trade sex for money, for example, are at heightened risk for adverse consequences of abuse and yet remain unaccounted for in the mainstream movement. The result is that these groups are left uniquely vulnerable to increased harm from relationships *and* from the state.

The Violence Against Women Act (VAWA) was situated within this landscape of mainstream anti-violence organizations garnering increasing state recognition and defining gender and sexual violence narrowly. Its reception was unsurprising. Of course, the state should "protect women," so few questioned the accompanying forms of carcerality that emerged and deepened. VAWA was the more visible facet of what Mimi Kim calls the "carceral creep" of the 1990s. As part of the Violent Crime Control and Law Enforcement Act (VCCLEA), better known as the 1994 Crime Bill, VAWA bolstered this erroneous framing of gender violence as requiring a criminal justice solution.[25] VCCLEA passed with wide bipartisan support and funneled tax dollars to policing and prison expansion. VAWA led to an influx of public and private funding and solidified state control over responses to gender violence. Mari Matsuda spoke out immediately after the passage of the 1994 Crime Bill as one of the few public critics of VAWA. Particularly concerned with the proliferation of federal death penalty offenses included in the VCCLEA, Matsuda wrote in *Ms.* magazine in 1994: "The challenge for feminists is to fight the patriarchal model that spawns racism, police brutality, corruption, and a value system of property before people."[26] Twenty years later, Mimi Kim described Matsuda as highlighting "the eerie silence from feminists seemingly willing to muffle any misgivings about collaboration with the criminal legal system under the thunder of self-congratulatory applause."[27]

Despite the outcry of women of color, lesbians, survivors, activists, and community organizers, the federalization of the response through the passage of VAWA created impermeable bureaucratic structures at the local, state, and national levels and a push for professionalization that completely coopted a once radical movement for safety and justice.

As Kim describes it, "Early social movement successes against an initially unresponsive criminal justice system evolved into collaborative relationships that altered the autonomy and constitution of initial social movement organizations."[28] Consider the simultaneity of the acceleration of other policies and systems that purported to address gender and sexual violence, like mandatory reporting requirements and the creation of sex offender registries, rescue-oriented programs for sex workers, statutory rape legislation, and domestic violence and other courts. By deploying rhetorical ruses about the generalized vulnerability of (particular) women and children, the omnipresent risk to individuals (rather than structural violence), and the capacity of the state to deliver benevolent (paternalistic) safety, the mainstream anti-violence movement uncritically accepted carcerality as the solution to what women of color activists had long argued was a social justice problem for which the state was partially culpable. If state violence and gender violence are inseparable, the corresponding explosion of carceral "solutions" augmented harm and created more dangerous circumstances for survivors of violence. It is here, where conservative responses to gender violence became absorbed into the popular rhetoric of carcerality and the concomitant buildup of a prison nation, that we most clearly see the trajectory of a movement veering toward what has come to be called carceral feminism—in direct political opposition to abolition feminism.[29]

Carceral feminism refers to an overreliance on carceral approaches to solve the problem of gender violence, despite research that clearly establishes that the carceral regime harms Black and other people of color and other marginalized groups. Asserting that the criminal legal system has the potential and obligation to "protect victims of violence," carceral feminism authorizes the state to use laws and law enforcement to legitimately exercise power: the state judges and controls behaviors deemed "bad," defining as "bad" those who engage in criminal acts. This framework assumes that gender oppression is a common experience, primarily a problem of individual cisgender men using violence against cisgender women, and that the state should intervene by increasing policing, making legislative changes, creating new laws and arrest policies, prosecuting more people, expanding imprisonment, and implementing other carceral strategies. The result is not safety or justice but the greater criminalization of marginalized groups.

We emphasize the simultaneity of the evolution of radical abolitionist consciousness and mainstream trends in gender violence work: as critiques of incarceration moved into the mainstream, so did critiques of mainstream responses to gender violence. A wider public became familiar with mass incarceration and sexual assault, physical and verbal, because of many decades of persistent and often unrecognized organizing in both areas. Gender violence became recognized as the most pandemic form of violence in the world but was also understood in decontextualized individualistic terms. As attention is most often focused on individual perpetrators, as if they themselves are the beginning and end of these violences, the structural and institutional underpinnings of sexual assault and other forms of gender violence are neglected. This is an unfortunate example of the failure to learn from struggles against racism: remaining at the level of the individual will compel endless repetition of legal and other proceedings in efforts implicitly predicated on the impossibility of purging our societies of these harms. In this way, the perpetual reliance on structures of policing was guaranteed.

Critical Interventions

Women of color feminist activists spent years trying to disrupt patterns in the individualization of violence and the resultant investment in the criminal legal system. Around the turn of the millennium, a series of gatherings produced position papers and statements forecasting the deleterious impact that overreliance on the criminal legal system would have on anti–gender violence work. One noteworthy example is a 2001 paper by Annanya Bhattacharjee entitled "Whose Safety? Women of Color and the Violence of

A button distributed in 2019 by Project Nia, based on a quote by Mariame Kaba.

Law Enforcement" and published by the American Friends Service Committee.[30] As one of the first *direct* challenges to overreliance on the carceral state in the new millennium, "Whose Safety?" considered human rights and reproductive and environmental justice from within an anti–gender violence framework in a decidedly abolitionist feminist way. Bhattacharjee asked provocatively, "What does it mean in practice to fight violence against women while simultaneously addressing the structural violence faced by the larger community?" Or, as we formulate the question today, how to acknowledge the structural character of gender violence alongside its intersections with violences generated by racism and capitalism.

Of course, the very posing of such questions builds on generations of previous work, such as that by white antiracist community organizer Anne Braden in the last century and turn-of-the twentieth century anti-lynching activist Ida B. Wells, that challenged the state's failed carceral engagements that purported to "protect" women (specifically white women).[31] Black feminist intellectuals and community-based activists have relentlessly attempted to articulate gender violence with anti-Black racism. Because the very history of the United States proceeds from the noxious interrelatedness of colonialism and slavery, anti-Black racism and racist violence directed against Indigenous people have always involved mutually connected systems. As Indigenous feminist scholar-activists have pointed out that sexual violence was an indispensable tool of colonial violence, so have Black feminists explored similar dynamics under slavery—and these insights further entail acknowledging the entangled histories of imperialism and gender/sexual violence. In short, any attempt to theorize violence directed at women and gender nonbinary people must go beyond addressing interpersonal violence to ending forms of violence from the state. Thus, projects undertaken by many feminist-of-color organizations have involved arguing that gender oppression is central to an understanding of racist violence and that conversely, white supremacy is central to an understanding of gender violence. Capitulating to a carceral feminism that calls upon the state to "protect" women from gender violence would replicate the very conditions that needed to be challenged.

While *carceral feminism* is a relatively new term, the turn to the state that it describes is not at all new. This is precisely one of the reasons why women of color have been historically hesitant to identify with feminism. The harm that is produced and reproduced through endless cycles of reform continues as mainstream anti-violence leaders stubbornly address gender violence in isolation, disconnect it from other forms of injustice, and reject attention to racist and other forms of state violence. Addressing attempts at reform that inevitably fail, abolition feminism challenges the ideological conceptualization of safety and protection as achievable through the state's punitive authority. It therefore creates new terrains of struggle: for access to resources for community development, mutual aid, or healing, and it creates new analytical and material spaces to imagine and experiment with more authentic forms of safety. Carceral policies creep into institutions and practices without any rational measure of effectiveness and therefore produce multiple sites and openings for abolition feminist engagements that are *actually focused on ending gender violence, in all its forms.*[32] Yet as commitments to abolition feminism grow, questions about the contours of reform persist. Indeed, "freedom is a constant struggle," and we must both be patient with ourselves and have high expectations of our work.[33] To do so allows us to remember to embrace experimentation and complexity, and to practice optimism and hope as we grow our abolition feminist organizations and praxis.

These reconceptualizations of safety require understanding that the pretext of ending gender violence allows the state to determine the nature of the problem, to decide on "reasonable" solutions, and to categorize people as either deserving to be free from injury or not. These are the same tactics that people who cause harm in intimate relationships use: arbitrary authority, attribution of blame to justify punishment, and expulsion of those who are objectionable, threatening, or obsolete. Monica Cosby, a Chicago-based abolition feminist, forcefully argues that prison is quite literally a form of gender violence. In both instances, harm results from the arbitrary use of authority, the abuse of power with impunity, the absolute control of bodies, minds, and spirits of survivors, as well as the way that the impact of both gender violence and imprisonment are ignored or minimized. People who suffer from both are blamed for their condition, and re-victimization is common. The criminal legal system so profoundly masks the harm that it produces that even when people are not helped by the system, the system is never held responsible for its failings and the individual is instead at fault. Cosby further argues that prisons cause the social death of women who are incarcerated by dehumanizing them, stripping them of their rights, and making them invisible behind barbed wire and brick walls. In a 2020 discussion, "Prison Is Abuse," Cosby adapted an image that was widely circulated by anti-violence organizers, the Power and Control Wheel, to reflect an abolition feminist analysis of gender violence. Based on her experience while incarcerated, she created the *Intimate Partner Violence and State Violence Power and Control Wheel*. Cosby illustrated the connection between interpersonal and state violence by describing a shakedown, or raid on a person's cell where personal property is destroyed, which crystalized her analysis of this relationship:

> If there is anybody out there who has never been in prison, but understands violent relationships, it is the same. Just because he (the guard) was insulted, he retaliated against us and I ended up in solitary (confinement). It just kind of clicked. And I think it had been knocking around in my head for a while that what was happening to me inside (the prison) was what happens in violent relationships.

PRISON IS
GENDER VIOLENCE

Emotional Abuse
makes them feel bad about themselves, calls names ; makes them think they are crazy, humiliates

Intimidation and Stalking
makes them feel afraid; damages their property, displays weapons

Coercion and Threats
carries out threats to harm; threatens to report them to other agencies

Economic Abuse
prevents them from working, makes them ask for money; takes their money

Uses Privileges
treats them like a servant; makes all the big decisions; uses stereotypes against them

Minimizing, Denying and Blaming
makes light of abuse shifts blame for abuse saying they caused it

Isolation
controls where they go, what they do, what they read, limits work and activities

Uses Children
makes them feel guilty about children; uses visitation to harass; threatens to take the children away

power and control

Emotional Abuse
makes them feel bad about themselves, infantilizes them calls names ; makes them think they are crazy, humiliates

Intimidation and Stalking
shakes down their cells, strip searches, displays weapons, mandatory supervised release/parole and electronic monitoring

Coercion and Threats
threatens to call the tactical team, threatens to lose visits or programming, threatens with segregation

Economic Abuse
exploitative prison labor; extortion of commissary prices; controls how they can spend and who can give money

Uses Privileges
enforces arbitrary rules; forced to follow any and all officer rules, constant surveillance of self and property

Minimizing, Denying and Blaming
retaliation for making grievances; says they are in prison for "their own good"

Isolation
controls who they can visit, who they can talk to by phone, reads their mail, uses solitary confinement

Uses Children
threatens to take visits away; holds DCFS programming against them; separation from children; threat of permanent separation from children

intimate partner violence

state violence

FREE ALL SURVIVORS

Monica Cosby's *Intimate Partner Violence and State Violence Power and Control Wheel*, illustrated by Sarah Ross (see appendices for full text).

Cosby described how her firsthand experiences of abuse and incarceration felt the same to her: prisoners are forced to yield to the rules and regulations of prisons lest they are punished with violence, just as survivors of violence, as she stated, "find themselves at the mercy of their abusive partner."

Cosby's insight was preceded by a similar analysis of state violence that emerged in the work of Sisters Inside, an organization in

Queensland, Australia, for incarcerated and formerly incarcerated women. Sisters Inside centers women with lived experiences of imprisonment to produce more complex understandings of both interpersonal and state violence, as well as more capacious conceptions of feminism that frame gender, race, sexuality, and ability as reciprocally interacting. In 2001, Sisters Inside developed an important and inventive campaign against what they termed state sexual assault. This campaign ("Stop State Sexual Assault!") represented the state as an agent of sexual violence, especially when it came to invasive but routine strip searches and cavity searches, and was based on a theorization of gender violence that linked individual and institutional violence, intimate and state violence. Currently and formerly incarcerated women pointed out that physical and sexual abuse by partners and other individuals did not feel any different from abuse behind walls. This abolition feminist campaign and its internationalist framework reconceptualized the relationship between state violence and individualized sexual violence. Sisters Inside also recognizes the ongoing violence of colonialization, and as it challenges the prison industrial complex, it works toward aboriginal self-determination. This reframing of safety within a decolonial frame is an important example of the organizing vision of abolition feminism.

Ongoing Movements, Familiar Tensions

Contemporary uprisings have surfaced familiar tensions: urgent organized calls to defund the police are met with cautious resistance from advocates who express concern for "women who have been sexually assaulted" or "people who need protection from abusive partners" and require emergency intervention. Despite the vibrant landscape of abolition feminist organizing and the powerful interventions across decades like the Moment of Truth and the INCITE!-Critical Resistance statements, the current political moment echoes an earlier carceral nightmare when anti–gender violence activists reinvested in law-and-order politics. The uprisings against police violence that took place in the spring and summer of 2020 created an opportunity for feminist anti-violence organizations to resist, to organize, to make visible the violence of the state, but it also created an opportunity to consolidate and deepen existing forms of state power.

Each new iteration of federal and state laws ostensibly designed to "protect" vulnerable women and girls also represents potential concessions to carceral responses, framing carceral creep as inevitable.[34] In the same way that struggles for accountability from the state for one "killer cop" can deflect attention away from the omnipresent violence of policing, concerns about what to do with the serial rapist or the long-term domestic abuser are put forth as a reality check for overly optimistic abolitionists and to illustrate their dismissal of gender violence. Of course, these are not new political predicaments: contemporary tensions between those working to liberate Black lives and those committed to gender justice echo earlier dynamics.

The current iteration of this familiar tension over demands to move away from carceral solutions ignores the important evidence that policing and punishment do not reduce overall rates of gender violence even as they may provide some short-term relief

from a crisis. This critique of the demand to defund or shift resources away from law enforcement assumes that the institution
of policing has the capacity and the will to resolve gender violence.
At the most basic level, advocates of carceral reforms suggest that
abolitionist approaches are "anti-victim," ignoring the reality that
police are *trained* to use force rather than to prevent or address
root causes of violence, which is perhaps why police officers are
more likely to engage in violent behavior with their partners than
other groups.[35]

Furthermore, the short-term relief associated with state
arrest and punishment is not always (or even usually) what
survivors of violence want; it does not involve them in decision-making as to what they need and seldom restores what they
lost. Slightly less than half of all incidents of intimate partner
violence are reported to the police; there are even fewer sexual
assaults reported. Black, Indigenous, and other women of color,
trans people, people in queer relationships, immigrant wom-
en, disabled people, children—those who are arguably most at
risk of intimate, stranger, Child Protective Services, police and
prison violence—are even less likely to seek assistance from the
carceral state. As Leigh Goodmark, a University of Maryland
law professor (whose Twitter name as of 2021 is "Recovering
Carceral Feminist-Ask Me How!") and major proponent of de-
criminalizing gender violence, argues, "Now we know it doesn't
work. We have the data that shows involvement in the criminal
legal system does not deter intimate partner violence, does not
lower rates of intimate partner violence, and it does not make
violence less severe."[36]

SELF DEFENSE IS NOT A CRIME

support trans women of color

In 2012, EISHA LOVE, a young Black trans woman, was attacked by a group of men. She accidentally injured one of them while trying to escape. She was arrested and spent nearly 4 years in a men's jail without a trial, because she could not afford bail.

Portrait of Eisha Love, who was incarcerated for defending herself and spent nearly four years in jail because she couldn't afford bail, by Micah Bazant.

Abolition feminism teaches us that gender violence is a complicated social issue with deep cultural roots and has been incorporated by the mainstream into the larger carceral project. Turning to punishment agencies and tactics of social control will not protect women and others harmed by gender violence. Survivors of violence would be much more likely to benefit if the over eight billion dollars spent on VAWA between 1995 and 2018 supported free and subsidized services like safe permanent housing, education, accessible health and mental health care, high-quality childcare, and job training and employment placement, in addition to collective and environmental assets such as neighborhood services that promote health and well-being, safe parks, healthy food options, cultural and arts activism, and mutual aid projects.[37]

Even as the backlash to the call for defunding the police deploys gender violence as a smokescreen, abolition feminist engagements with gender-based harm—often unfolding at a different register and on a different timetable—continue to alter the landscape. For example, Black queer feminist organizational initiatives work to create everyday forms of safety outside of policing. Both the Audre Lorde Project's Safe Outside the System initiative and the Black Youth Project (BYP) 100's She Safe, We Safe campaign aim to "shift culture and establish new ways of keeping each other safe within our communities AND work to fight against the violence of the state, particularly the patriarchal violence of the police."[38] Survived & Punished supports women who have been criminalized in freeing themselves from the aftereffects of incarceration, partly through community education on violence prevention—one means of creating a softer landing and welcoming criminalized survivors home from prison. In 2020 the Movement for Black Lives organized ongoing strategic discussions on patriarchal violence in an attempt to fully integrate abolition feminist work into its political agenda.

At the same time, broader state coalitions—organizations once funded by federal agencies—are also calling for abolitionist alternatives. Spurred by the Moment of Truth statement, the California Partnership to End Domestic Violence, the National Coalition of Anti-Violence Programs, and an emerging network of more radical state anti-violence coalitions are reflecting on their own collusion with the carceral state and shifting to invest in practices that address gender violence while not increasing vulnerability to the violence of the carceral state. Motivated by the need to correct the course of anti-violence work, these initiatives span from creating alternatives to calling 911 and developing new funding streams to explicitly changing laws that criminalize or encourage overpolicing.

Dorothy Roberts persuasively argues for an expansion of the frame of abolition to include the violence of the foster care system and what she calls the family policing system. Issues related to institutions that are frequently referred to as "children's protective services" contribute to the normalization of carceral responses as the only means of addressing the social problems experienced by poor Black families and other families of color ensconced in poverty. When, for example, the presence of rats in an apartment is used as evidence for the initiation of proceedings to "protect" the children by removing them from their family, it is the mother or parent who is considered culpable and penalized by having her chidren removed. Neither the landlord nor the larger social system is assigned responsibility. According to Roberts,

> The abolitionist mission to liberate Black people from captivity must include freeing family caregivers from state surveillance and children from foster care. Ultimately, movements to dismantle different parts of the carceral state are working toward

the same world—a world where all children are safe and cared
for without the need for police, prisons, and family separation.
A more expansive understanding of policing and abolition that
contests the state's benevolent terror is essential to collectively
building a new society that supports rather than destroys families and communities.[39]

In Australia, Flat Out, an organization by and for women
in the criminal legal system in Melbourne, drew attention to
how prisons and systems of child and family services create
more harm but represent themselves as mitigating domestic violence.[40] In 2019, spurred by the deaths of people in jails across
Australia, particularly Indigenous women, Sisters Inside started a crowdsourcing campaign, #FreeHer, to raise money to post
bail for the release of Indigenous and other women in prison,
who are often arrested and imprisoned for small unpaid debts.
Sisters Inside raised over $300,000 and made visible in the pro-
cess the open secret of the fundamentally capitalist and colonial
roots of the prison industrial complex.[41] These creative efforts
are building in many parts of the world. In Black townships outside of Johannesburg, queer and trans women have developed
safety patrols and are slowly organizing broader systems of support in their communities.[42]

This abolition feminism ecosystem is rarely mapped, formally named, or recognized as part of a wider internationalist movement. Sisters Uncut, a survivor-led, radical feminist organization,
bases its work on an internationalist and intersectional understanding of how gender violence produces and reinforces state
violence and of how abolition feminism demands social transfor-

Poster by Centre for the Human Rights of Imprisoned People working group, a project of Flat Out, created in 2015.

mation as the only means to ensure safety for survivors. Taking visible positions of solidarity, in 2020 Sisters Uncut issued a statement in support of the Wet'suwet'en people of Turtle Island (in the region known as British Columbia, Canada):

> From the belly of the colonial beast, Sisters Uncut stands in solidarity with those on the frontlines and with Indigenous people everywhere in the global fight against empire. We recognize the direct links between gendered, white supremacist and colonial violence. We fight colonialism in all its forms, including its imposition of patriarchal structures and the gender binary. We support the fight of the Wet'suwet'en people and their history-making resistance movement, a movement where Indigenous women hold leadership.[43]

Abolition feminism requires a respect for movements toward self-determination, recognizing forms of oppression across borders as an important context for redefining both anti-violence work and freedom.[44]

FREE MARISSA

In 2013, the Chicago Alliance to Free Marissa Alexander used this image by Molly Crabapple in their efforts to support and free Marissa Alexander, a mother who was criminalized and imprisoned for defending herself against her abusive husband. After Marissa reached a plea deal in 2015, CAFMA transitioned into Love & Protect.

III.

Now.

It is April 10, 2020, and ample early spring sunshine across meadows almost obscures the reality: this is a car caravan circling a prison during a pandemic. Almost one month into the statewide "shelter in place" order in Illinois—before George Floyd, before Breonna Taylor, before Tony McDade—and with twelve COVID-19 related deaths reported, Stateville prison in Crestville is a national hot spot, like many other prisons across the country. The National Guard is overseeing medical services, masks and hand sanitizer are scant, and people inside are on 24-hour lockdown. As the virus accelerated in early spring 2020 with increased infections and reports of death, family members, loved ones, and grassroots community-based organizations moved with urgency to push for people's release. Despite demands for furlough, compassionate release, and clemency, no one from this maximum-security prison for people the state designates as men, with a population of approximately 3,500 people, has been released. While COVID-19's lethality in confined spaces reportedly led to action in other places—Indonesia, Iran, and India—

Untitled by Joseph Dole. A writer, artist, and activist, Joe is one of the first incarcerated people in the state of Illinois to earn an undergraduate degree in decades, which he completed in 2018. He is also the cofounder of Parole Illinois and a member of the Prison + Neighborhood Arts / Education Project.

relatively few people were released from US state prisons over the course of the pandemic despite the vibrancy of a movement to defund the police.[1]

The caravan gets scraggly because of the length of the journey—it takes about fifteen minutes to make a full circle around the prison, which commands an impressive 2,200 acres. The cars follow a truck towing a giant speaker blasting music and a thirty-minute Zoom program that includes prerecorded comments from people inside who describe the situation as desperate. The names of the known dead are read. Key organizers—formerly incarcerated women—also testify. This multiracial caravan consists largely of women, children and young people, and queer people. As many in the caravan are regular visitors to this prison—loved ones, educators, attorneys—it feels exhilarating to circle in cars decorated with signs: *Release Them All! Abolition Now!* Perhaps anticipating an insurgency, the prison blocks every entrance with law enforcement vehicles and armed officers. During the pandemic, car caravans like these—circling prisons, jails, and other detention centers—erupted all over the country.

Premature death from COVID-19 galvanized these demands, and yet people were always already dying too early in prisons.[2] Medical neglect, overcrowding, bad food, cramped cells, limited access to condoms, and communal eating lead to preventable and infectious diseases, including hepatitis, HIV, and diabetes. Cruel and exploitative conditions, like price gouging in the commissary and in telecommunications, along with the scarcity of soap, menstrual supplies, and toilet paper, are all normalized conditions.[3] Before COVID-19 eighty to a hundred people were dying every year in Illinois prisons according to data the state was forced to make publicly available. This number does not include casualties from the approximately 250,000 times people cycle through Illinois's ninety-two county jails, or the count from federal prisons and other detention centers. Incarceration itself has always been a pandemic.

The emergency response to the outbreak of the pandemic in Illinois was organized by groups composed largely of women of color, queer folks, and young people. Leading up to the caravan, this informal network called the planning meetings, made the agendas, took the notes, knitted the relationships, hustled the meager resources required, held down the day's logistics, and instigated the action debriefs. This reflects the pre-pandemic reality: the waiting room at the prison was always full of mothers, wives, lovers, sisters, daughters. The women who waited to visit now helped to organize car caravans, deliver emergency supplies, and call for *decarceration now!* Although some of those circling the prison that day identify as abolitionists and as feminists, this work is not widely recognized as feminist, even gendered, labor. What are the costs of this erasure, this failure to make visible and to name feminism's indivisibility from abolition?

Fast-forward several months in 2020 to another crisis, another mobilization, more labor and action: on the July 4th weekend in Chicago, with a COVID-19 quarantine still in effect, hundreds of people turned out in person for defund Chicago Police Department mass resistance trainings. With a social media call to show up for "an orientation to police/prison abolition" and a discussion of "how we are going to defund the police in Chicago, and how we can use organizing, direct action, and movement building to win," this weekend was organized just days in advance by a new collective that mobilized almost overnight, the Black Abolitionist Network (BAN). The four-hour sessions on each day of the long weekend—an outdoor event with physical distancing, masks, and hand sanitizer—centered accessibility in a range of ways that included providing excellent food, free childcare, breaks, and sign language interpretation. Located in neighborhoods across Chicago while the mercury was rising, these trainings, with many young queer Black women running operations and workshops, were booked out almost immediately. From cleaning the empty lots where the trainings were held to creating a dynamic that encouraged visionary thinking, organizers created space for imagining a different world. Like the car caravan around Stateville prison, Chicago's July 4th weekend was abolition feminism at work.

In the summer of 2020 sustained public demands to disinvest, shrink, or abolish (not reform) policing and for *abolition now!* emerged after decades of practice, experimentation, and critical assessment. These forms of praxis and collective engagement do the slow work both of deconstruction, or a critique and disavowal of the carceral state, and the labor of a productive experimentation, the creation and engagement with fresh tools and a shared analysis/language. These years also proliferated our ability to dream audaciously: as feminist writer and organizer Gloria Anzaldúa wrote in 1987, "Nothing happens in the 'real' world unless it first happens in the images in our heads."[4] Over time, these varied manifestations of abolition feminism deepened our collective imagination: the state does not offer the solution to interpersonal violence, and existing forms of state "protection," including police, prisons, and social welfare programs, create more violence and harm. Collective formations of abolition feminism—ad hoc and formal—from the Combahee River Collective to Sisters Uncut, from the germinal anti-violence work of the National Black Women's Health Project to the founding of INCITE!—continue to build daily responses to a wide range of harms while working to challenge systemic and structural forms of state violence. These small networks—some persisting across decades—exemplify the practice and the politics of abolition feminism.

Turning to the everydayness of one site, Chicago, this chapter engages with the last two decades of abolitionist feminist organizing and the daily and collective experiments of living otherwise. Yet Chicago is not exceptional. There are multiple chapters to be written about Johannesburg, Montreal, Seattle, and many other sites. However, we argue that even a partial focus on the everydayness of a particular location offers the opportunity to both surface the power of small, hyperlocal, and sometimes fleeting actions and networks, and to map and archive the ongoing, cumulative, and collective impact of these (often tiny) formations. Insisting on attention to now defunct organizations, largely forgotten campaigns, highly local events, and small collectives, this chapter illuminates the rich historical movement of abolition feminism as a method.

Abolition feminist practices and analyses did not grow by scaling up or through institutionalized forms of power. Predicated on sameness and often eradicating difference, scaling up can foreclose transformation.[5] A close engagement with one site suggests that an

Sounds of Abolition by Monica Trinidad, created in collaboration with incarcerated people through the People's Paper Co-op in 2021.

abolition feminist ecology emerges from everyday practices, collective experiments driven by necessity, practice, and reflection, and in sinewy networks that crisscross time and space. Far from utopian, this world is ready at hand, already underway. As the lawyer and organizer Bryan Stevenson stated in part of a 2020–2021 series of virtual artistic and political engagements titled Visualizing Abolition, the presence of something different is palpable: "I just believe there's something better waiting for us. I do believe there is something that feels more like freedom, more like equality, more like justice, waiting for us. For all of us."[6] As a history of Chicago's present, and with an ear for the notes at the margins, this chapter aims to chronicle and advance local practices that not only demand but mobilize something better. *Now* is the time to build, to practice, and, yes, to study. *Now* is the imperative to name how feminism is central to abolition and abolition is indivisible from our feminism.

Violence of Policing

On November 24, 2015, Chicago was again in the streets over the death of another Black youth, seventeen-year-old Laquan McDonald, at the hands of a white police officer. More than a year earlier Laquan McDonald had been shot sixteen times by Jason Van Dyke. Initially ruled a "justifiable homicide," the dashcam footage of the entire incident, suppressed both by the blue wall of silence and by complicit city officials, was released only after thirteen months of relentless pressure from independent journalists, Laquan McDonald's family, and a network of small, community-based organizations. The footage was devastating: thirty seconds after he arrived at the scene, Van Dyke fired his gun at McDonald, who was not lunging toward the police but running away.

Until recently, the varied forms of police violence and their familiar targets—Black and brown people, poor people, queers, labor organizers, sex workers, migrants—rarely made headlines. The police killings of Native Americans, the most likely of any racial or ethnic group to be killed by US law enforcement, still rarely receive mainstream media coverage.[7] The National Center for Transgender Equality's US Transgender Survey reported in 2015 that 58 percent of those surveyed who had contact with police or law enforcement officers reported some form of mistreatment.[8] Also made invisible is the "slow violence" of how other carceral entities such as social services police bodies, targeting poor women who are overwhelmingly Black and Indigenous—for example, in mandated and random drug tests for meager social assistance benefits like Temporary Assistance for Needy Families (TANF). Policing—in its varied forms—has always been a pandemic.

Chicago has deep histories of resistance to this ongoing violence of policing.[9] Just a few years before Laquan McDonald's death, in 2012, the network We Charge Genocide raised the visibility of another young Black person killed by a white police officer, twenty-two-year-old Rekia Boyd. The group demanded measures of accountability beyond prosecution, and in 2014 We Charge Genocide submitted a shadow or unofficial report to the United Nations, *Police Violence Against Chicago's Youth of Color*, documenting the fact that police officers regularly engaged in torture.[10] Among their twenty recommendations, We Charge

Genocide insisted on defining and creating safety outside of a carceral framework and building alternatives to policing and imprisonment. By 2015 the response to Laquan McDonald's death and the police coverup felt different from previous uprisings in response to the violence of policing. While calls to prosecute Jason Van Dyke surfaced immediately and the chants in the street were familiar, "No Justice, No Peace, No Racist Police," different strategies and demands for accountability and transformation gained traction. With almost 40 percent of Chicago's operating budget already earmarked for policing (15 percent of the city's total budget including grants), in a political moment when austerity logic justified the closure of public schools and public mental health centers in Black and brown neighborhoods, a network of grassroots activists pushed not to prosecute but to shrink the footprint of policing.[11] In the wake of Laquan McDonald's death, the demand to fund Black futures and to divest from policing as a pathway to safety and accountability resonated across new audiences. This was abolition feminism in practice.

The outrage in Chicago over the murder of Laquan McDonald echoed across the country, accentuating the fact that everywhere, from New York City to Ferguson to Minneapolis, police kill with impunity. State violence also plays out in other ways, targeting women, trans people, and gender nonconforming people. In the rare cases when state violence is made visible, accountability is thinly individuated: the problem is a discrete incident, a specific officer. In 2015 former Oklahoma City police officer Daniel Holtzclaw was convicted of raping thirteen Black women. In 2020, two police officers in Kansas City, Missouri, were indicted after assaulting Brianna (BB) Hill on a city side-walk.[12] While these prosecutions are rare and convictions rar-er, policing is a key mechanism of state violence: the murders of Breonna Taylor, Tony McDade, Sandra Bland, and thousands of other Black and Indigenous women and queer and trans people, are grim evidence of the misogynist and transphobic character of policing, which, alongside racism, is expressed in the murder of cisgender men of color.[13] Given this landscape, anti-violence organizers and scholars worked to critically examine the gen-dered and heterosexist dimensions of the violence of policing.

Noteworthy among these efforts is the #SayHerName cam-paign organized and led by professor Kimberlé Crenshaw of the African American Policy Forum (AAPF). Since releasing the orig-inal May 2015 "Say Her Name: Resisting Police Brutality against Black Women" report, AAPF has been documenting the specific ways that Black women, girls, femmes, and trans people are targets of violent policing and how silence creates further danger for wom-en who are outside of the gaze of most anti-violence and racial jus-tice activists. From holding public tribunals to coproducing a song by Janelle Monáe, AAPF has challenged the movement to include the names—and therefore never forget the lives—of Black women killed by police.

One key difference in this moment of police violence is that camera phones and social media now document and amplify some of the more recent and egregious instances of state violence. The poet Elizabeth Alexander describes the "Trayvon Gener-ation," the young people who are growing up watching these murder clips on their phones, "on the school bus," "under covers," "crisscrossed and concentrated."[14] These graphic, real-time assaults, coupled with growing calls for police accountability, sometimes translate into attempts to sanction law enforcement or to implement "new" measures of police surveillance, including body cameras.[15] Yet the demands for police accountability emanating from the 2020 uprisings increasingly hinged not on reforms but on abolitionist calls to divest from the carceral state through critical dialogue: while we know that prosecution and the state will not protect us, what do we do with the killer cops, the rapist cops, and the transphobic cops that white supremacy and heteropatriarchy produce and protect? Jason Van Dyke was charged with first-degree murder in Chicago on the day the video footage was finally released. Three other police officers, including his partner, were also charged with conspiracy to cover up Laquan McDonald's murder.

While there are undoubtedly individual police officers who are racist and transphobic, systems and institutions empower, educate, reproduce, validate, and arm these individual actors. Yet if the criminal legal system is barely equipped to indict its own employees, it is completely unable to critically examine and indict its own structure. With approximately twenty civilian complaints in Van Dyke's personnel record largely related to the use of excessive force—an above average number of complaints for a Chicago police officer—none resulted in any disciplinary action. Through another lens, Van Dyke was neither particularly exceptional nor an outlier. He was just caught.

Feminist Genealogies

Seventeen years before Laquan McDonald was murdered and a decade before Rekia Boyd was killed, communities across Chicago were organizing—by necessity—to build and define safety outside of policing. We draw attention to the Young Women's Empowerment Project (YWEP), which started in 2002 and closed in 2013, as a self-described "social justice organizing project that is led by and for young people of color who have current or former experience in the sex trade and street economies."[16] With a mantra of "we are not the problem—we are the solution" and a practice of mutual aid and harm reduction, YWEP's highly local organizing highlighted how state entities charged with protecting young people, including social workers and police, are a primary source of danger and harm for street-based young people. YWEP's popular education campaigns focused on safer sex, needle/syringe exchanges, free and affirming health care, DIY legal support, and access to free food and technology. From inception, their political education materials, campaigns, and public events functioned to educate (and often alarm) other groups working with young people in the street economy.

YWEP was preceded by and sometimes overlapped with a cluster of local feminist anti-violence networks that coalesced in response to everyday forms of gender and sexual violence. These formations, including A Long Walk Home, Mango Tribe, Aqua-Moon, GABRIELA Network Chicago, Ella's Daughters, Females United for Action, Girl Talk, Women and Girls Collective Action Network, Female Storytellers Igniting Revolution to End Violence, and the Rogers Park Young Women's Action Team, centered the violence experienced by young women of color, including street harassment, sexual assault, racism, transphobia, and homophobia.[17] Recognizing that families, schools, and policing do not offer support or protection, and that harm is not individual and private but endemic and ideologically sustained, these networks (both ad hoc and formal, both autonomous and attached to existing larger organizations) demanded not simply services or recognition but structural and systemic change. In tandem with the ongoing national dialogues outlined in chapter two, these forms of organizing and direct action often tied racism, ableism, and capitalism to gender and sexual violence, and moved beyond simply indicting individual perpetrators to offering pathways for communities and neighborhoods to imagine and develop collective responses to gender and sexual violence. While very few of these Chicago-based anti-violence groups explicitly identified as abolitionist or even feminist during the early 2000s, their zines, spoken word events, street actions, and popular education workshops rejected the criminal legal system's ineffective response. Their work spotlighted the state's inability to recognize sexual and gender violence as harm, particularly when experienced by young people of color, including and especially those who are queer.[18]

Chicago was prepared to make different demands after Laquan McDonald's murder in part because of the labor and analysis of these preceding grassroots anti-violence networks. One key layer was the coalition in Chicago that built collaborative frameworks for restorative justice and for ending racist, ableist, and heterogendered disciplinary policies and practices in schools. Young people of color came together in cultural and political formations, including

Blocks Together, Southside Together Organizing for Power, South-west Youth Collaborative, and Batey Urbano, to force policymak-ers to pay attention to school pushout where policies and practices make it impossible for young people to stay in school. In 2006 two lawyers, Ora Schub and Cheryl Graves, started Community Justice for Youth Institute to generate restorative justice practices across the city. Schub and Graves are almost single-handedly responsible for training an entire generation of restorative justice practitioners in Chicago, and for creating openings for a wide range of people, in intimate contexts, to collectively dialogue and struggle around hard concepts like accountability and transformation.[19] In 2005, Community Organizing and Family Issues, a South Side organi-zation by and for Black family caregivers, overwhelmingly women, came together to challenge suspension and punishment policies in their neighborhood schools.[20] They created resources and trainings for adults to build free or low-cost restorative justice practices in schools that worked to stem the movement of young people of color into the criminal legal system.[21] Even though these organizations still train communities in radical "alternative" ideas and practices of safety, accountability, and transformation, the landscape that shapes and defines restorative justice has changed. As noted in an earlier chapter, the carceral system has coopted the language and some of the practices of restorative justice, disconnecting this work from its origins as a community-driven practice of accountability and transformation.

These practices of abolition feminism made visible and challenged both the state's failure to support women and other structurally vulnerable constituencies and the violence inherent in state-run (or state-supported) systems and institutions ostensibly designed to protect. In 2013, after years of organizing with young people like herself in the foster care system, Charity Tolliver started Chicago's Black on Both Sides (BOBS). BOBS worked to "highlight the voices and experiences of Black/African American foster youth while launching a direct action organizing campaign to address root causes of the foster care to prison pipeline." Through direct support for young people in the system and mothers and caregivers at risk of losing their children, BOBS supported campaigns and facilitated discussions and events to raise the visibility of the predatory nature of the family regulation system, and to build survival strategies for directly impacted women and young folks. BOBS explicitly supported two national and local campaigns against the expansion of mandated reporting and against laws that criminalize co-sleeping (when a caregiver, usually a mother, shares a bed with an infant/child). These are just two examples of how what Dorothy Roberts previously called the family regulation system, now also the family policing system, surveils and coerces caregivers and targets low-income mothers of color.[22] This system uses the language of child protection but in reality, does little to help vulnerable families with children, to reduce or eradicate violence toward children, or to create public dialogues about the structural contexts that facilitate harm.

Abolition feminism took root in these Chicago organizations challenging the family policing system but also in movements working to rethink the limited reformist demands of mainstream immigration movements. Local migrant justice organizations, particularly the Immigrant Youth Justice League established in

2009, came together to oppose migrant criminalization and deportation under the Bush and Obama administrations.[23] Shaped by their own experiences and also by emerging national and local contexts, many organizers began to reject the paltry legislative frameworks that rendered most people outside of the limited protection from deportation afforded by the DREAM Act.[24] Organizers began to center an analysis that did not cleave Immigration and Customs Enforcement from the prison industrial complex (as exemplified by the popular chants at the 2006 migrant justice marches in Chicago and across the US, "*Yo no soy criminal*"). New organizations emerged, such as Organized Communities Against Deportations, with an explicitly intersectional framework that centered the non-disposability of all migrant people.[25]

As Chicago cultivated a small but thriving landscape of grassroots organizations that began to identify explicitly as abolitionist, the language and analysis of abolition feminism proliferated and deepened, influenced by the national (and increasingly local) work of INCITE! and Critical Resistance. Chapters of INCITE! and Critical Resistance developed convenings, chapter actions, public statements, campaigns, and toolkits alongside Chicago Legal Advocacy for Incarcerated Mothers, particularly in the Visible Voices project, which centered the leadership, analysis, and public voice of women impacted by incarceration.[26] Ad hoc groups like Queer to the Left and GenderJUST developed creative anti-police direct actions and Project Nia created and distributed educational materials challenging the prison industrial complex and provided a wide range of workshops. The Chicago Dyke March Collective planned radical police-free celebrations. Women connected to people confined in the Illinois supermax prison at Tamms successfully agitated to shutter that prison. Young people inside and outside of the Cook County Juvenile Temporary Detention Center organized the Girl Talk Collective. The Transformative Justice Law Project offered do-it-yourself and mutual aid name change mobilizations as well as legal support by and for trans people impacted by the criminal legal system. Organized Communities against Deportation generated militant and public self-defense campaigns for people targeted for deportation.

These currents of feminist and abolitionist organizing both propelled new lines of inquiry and gave new traction to old demands. For example, this network insisted on the recognition of the state as a key perpetrator of violence and supported organizing that enabled new forms of visibility for racist police violence. For decades, groups had pushed for the city to be accountable for the violence of policing: between 1972 and 1991, more than a hundred Black men and at least one woman were subject to torture under Chicago police commander Jon Burge. A report to the United Nations Committee on the Elimination of Racial Discrimination detailed:

> The torture was intentionally inflicted to extract confessions, and techniques included electrically shocking men's genitals, ears and lips with cattle prods or an electric shock box, anally raping men with cattle prods, suffocating individuals with plastic bags, mock executions, and beatings with telephone books and rubber hoses.[27]

For decades many survivors of torture, along with their loved ones and affiliated Chicago organizations, worked relentlessly to expose the violence and the subsequent cover-ups and to free those convicted on false confessions. This network included the People's Law Office, Citizen's Alert, the Task Force to Confront Police Violence, the Aaron Patterson Defense Committee, the Campaign to End the Death Penalty, and Black People Against Torture.

This longstanding organizing was given fresh energy and tools from the abolitionist feminist ecosystems of We Charge Genocide, Project Nia, and other networks. Their labors, analyses, and interventions helped frame the most important victory in this movement—not Burge's conviction on charges of perjury and obstruction of justice in federal court but the unanimous passage of reparations legislation by the Chicago City Council in 2015 at the height of Black Lives Matter organizing. This legislation marked the first time a municipality voted explicitly to provide reparations for cases involving racist police violence. Moreover, the impressive organizing around police torture led to the involvement of many artists in a competition for a public memorial. Chicago Torture Justice Memorials continues to press the current mayor, Lori Lightfoot, to use the reparations legislation to fund the construction of the memorial. This organizing related to "police torture" expanded our analysis to recognize and center the "violence of policing"—far from being exceptional, as many marginalized communities, including sex workers, unhoused people, and young folks, intimately recognize, the everyday work of policing is regulation, coercion, and violence.

Emerging from this deepening analysis of overcriminalization as an artifact of state violence was the idea that torture and excessive force must be mapped on a continuum that included the

Logo of Love & Protect by Monica Trinidad.

criminalization of survivors of gender violence. More recent organizational foundations like Chicago's campaign-oriented activist group Love & Protect (and its national counterpart Survived & Punished) exist resolutely along that continuum, supporting survivors of gender violence and pushing for abolitionist engagements. Love & Protect outlines its mission to "support those who identify as women and gender non-conforming persons of color who are criminalized or harmed by state and interpersonal violence. Through love, we work towards healing and transformation with these individuals and their families. Through resistance, we seek to protect their right to defend themselves."[28]

Love & Protect redefines safety, proclaiming that "through love, through resistance, we protect!" In shifting the narrative, Love & Protect argues that survivors can only be defended by defunding the police: "Prisons do not support survivors, they punish survivors"—both because incarceration is not protective and as Monica Cosby and others suggest, prisons and detention centers are centralized locations of physical, sexual, and emotional abuse. Importantly, Love & Protect not only works on individual cases to set criminalized survivors free; it also produces political education materials designed to educate the public about what many survivors want and need: to build a culture (and a definition) of safety that does not rely on incarceration.[29]

Tackling the intimate and everyday violence experienced by those marked as disposable by the state, these organizations—forming an ecology of abolition feminism—continue to build essential tools, practices, languages, analyses, and mutual aid networks out of anger, love, and necessity. The accessible, free, and horizontal political education undertaken by these groups, often with few or no paid members and scant resources, continues to be breathtaking: the public convenings where people who are directly impacted shared analyses about how to intervene and interrupt the violence inflicted by the state; the many toolkits, safety labs, and workshops focused on how to address interpersonal harm without policing; the resources, services, and support for survivors, broadly conceived; the mutual aid initiatives to pool resources for rent, gender-affirming surgeries, bail, food, and parties; and the essays, books, articles, and blog posts that fleshed out how people foster accountability, healing, and transformation outside a carceral frame. The list of events, campaigns, resources, and workshops is endless: transformative justice and abolition workshops, a summer "comm-university" on the prison industrial complex, prison penpal meetups, reading and study groups, Saturday morning circles for formerly incarcerated people, film screenings of *Visions of Abolition*, *Out in the Night*, and *South-*

west of Salem, and safety labs that offer the opportunity to role-play how to intervene in everyday experiences of interpersonal harm without police. Sometimes joyous, always imperfect, and done with the expectation that change is relational and rarely immediate, these events and groups create the necessary conditions to imagine, practice, and strengthen abolition feminism. The lineage and the practice of this grassroots feminist ecosystem builds accountability and safety outside of law and order.

At times this slow work of building up our collective capacity to imagine and act in ways that do not expand the prison industrial complex has felt and continues to feel interminable. Messy. A kind of familiar yet chaotic beauty of a two-hour meeting that stretches into three. Or a circle where the introductions take far too long. Another spoken word performance. A version of the same crucial question from a participant—*What about the "really bad people"?* And despite this ecosystem, too many times the practices are not enough: for example, when one organizer sexually harms another organizer. Persisting even in the face of these urgent and heartbreaking contradictions, over the first two decades of the new millennium Chicago rehearsed and strengthened muscles and tools for a time to come. Dreamed up and carried out by women, nonbinary, and other queer people, this is the always urgent *slow time* of abolition.

Staying with the Trouble

These forms of experimentation are not without conflict and are always about risk. Pushing against dominant narratives and powerful institutions incurs backlash. People organize without health care and a living wage. People burn out. Many people struggle while facing their own experiences with violence and trauma. What we have learned, however, is that no time is the wrong time to organize, to assess movements, and to raise critical and challenging questions. Such organizing, which is often led by young feminists of color, frequently pushes necessary "other questions" to the forefront of abolitionist movements.

On April 1, 2016, before protests about Laquan McDonald's murder and before the need to caravan around a prison to raise the visibility of people inside dying of COVID, people were in the streets to resist another crisis. A city-wide march decrying two years of a budget crisis engineered by a Republican governor succeeded in shutting down Chicago. At the culminating rally, representatives from many of Chicago's key left social justice organizations—labor unions, anti-poverty groups, pro-migrant justice networks—spoke about their vision for a flourishing Chicago. Toward the end of the rally, Page May, a young adult organizer with the youth network Assata's Daughters, reminded audiences that while the budget impasse devastated communities, so too did the ongoing spectacle of Black death orchestrated by policing. From the stage she proclaimed, "Fuck the police, fuck CPD, fuck the FOP [Fraternal Order of Police]. . . . Fuck the police and everybody fuck with them."[30] May's comments immediately sparked scattered boos and cheers; despite the long history of CPD violence and racism, and despite the fact that the phrase had been popularized twenty-eight years earlier by N.W.A's song of the same name, she surprised many on the dais, including the organizers of the action, the Chicago Teachers Union (CTU) leadership.[31] Backlash was swift. Many attacked May personally, some with death threats, through social media and mainstream press outlets. Some participants in the rally distanced themselves immediately from her comments, and others, like the CTU, equivocated. What was obscured in the media was the asymmetry between the immense power held by police unions and one person yelling, *Fuck the police!*

The reaction to this comment revealed the necessity of challenging the power of carceral unions, particularly within labor and left organizing movements. Police unions wield enormous power and as Kristian Williams documents in *Our Enemies in Blue*, police "organize as *police*, not workers."[32] Likewise, when corrections officers mobilize politically, it is invariably for legislation, or in support of policymakers who advance "tough on crime" agendas. Their power is not inconsequential: the California Correctional Peace Officers Association is one of the most influential political action committees in the state.[33] The largest municipal police union in the nation is the 24,000-member Police Benevolent Association of New York.

The broader labor movement has rarely directly challenged the power of carceral unions, with few exceptions: in California, locals of the Service Employees International Union (SEIU) were persuaded to join the Coalition for Effective Public Safety (CEPS), a coalition formed more than a decade and half ago to push back on spending and other investments in corrections. While SEIU has members in California's prisons, ongoing abolitionist political education by members of CEPS—including Critical Resistance,

Justice Now, and A New Way of Life—convinced these SEIU locals that their survival and growth could not, and should not, be predicated on carcerality. By supporting this coalition, SEIU signaled that it understood that its workers' futures did not hinge on working in prison. In 2020, the AFL-CIO began cautious discussions about the role of organized labor in challenging "mass incarceration," but it has not ended its affiliation with the International Union of Police Associations or rejected the membership, or the dues, of policing and corrections unions.[34] The International Longshore and Warehouse Union should also be acknowledged for their consistent work over the years in support of political prisoner Mumia Abu-Jamal and for other challenges to carceral systems in the United States, South Africa, and occupied Palestine. More than any other union, they have embraced antiracist and abolitionist causes.

Some teachers' unions, pushed by decades of engineered austerity and grassroots organizing for restorative justice, are beginning to engage abolition. In Chicago, a district where 90 percent of students are students of color and 75 percent of schools are without a library, the Caucus of Rank and File Educators (CORE) brought new vigor to the Chicago Teachers Union in 2010 by centering the leadership and analysis of an intergenerational group of women of color, including the late and much-beloved Karen Lewis, who started the process of redefining the union as a force for collective social justice. Over the last decade the CTU has consistently strengthened ties of solidarity with Black and brown communities, created a culture of internal and external political education, rejected privatization, and centered the needs and visions of workers and communities of color. In the most recent contract negotiation process, the CTU engaged in what the city administration attempted to demean and trivialize as "bargaining for the public good"—demanding sanctuary schools (no ICE presence), affordable housing, and nurses and libraries in every public school. The CTU's vision resonated with families, communities, and workers, leading to two successful strikes in 2012 and 2019.

While the CTU's demands foregrounded aspects of what we might call an abolitionist agenda even though the union does not describe itself in these terms, May's comments pushed key questions to the surface. Yet mainstream media coverage focused primarily on May's anger. Why did she have to say, "Fuck the police"? This turn to respectability politics to disqualify dissonant, radical, and critical standpoints is not new.[35] Displays of anger and other "outlaw emotions" as Audre Lorde described them are frequently used against radical activists, particularly women of color.[36] This focus on affect justifies the erasure of the core message by focusing on the tone or mode of delivery. As Lorde observed,

> I have seen situations where white women hear a racist remark, resent what has been said, become filled with fury, and remain silent because they are afraid. That unexpressed anger lies within them like an undetonated device, usually to be hurled at the first woman of Color who talks about racism.
>
> But anger expressed and translated into action in the service of our vision and our future is a liberating and strengthening act of clarification, for it is in the painful process of this translation that we identify who are our allies with whom we have grave differences, and who are our genuine enemies.[37]

This moment offers another reminder both that our organizing must take on questions that some perceive to be uncomfortable and also that our work must open up pathways for people to flourish. Prisons, jails, and police are always hiring and yet Chicago fires teachers (disproportionately Black educators) and closes public schools in Black and brown neighborhoods.[38] No one hires poets and artists, yet resources are seemingly always available for surveillance cameras and school police. This form of *organized abandonment*, to use the term coined by David Harvey, and extensively developed by Ruth Wilson Gilmore, maps how environments are shaped to create optimal and flexible conditions for capital and are intentionally challenging to recognize.[39] Lead by women of color, the CORE caucus of the Chicago Teachers Union is beginning to tackle these questions and by example is pushing labor unions to confront the naturalization of policing in our communities. Creating opportunities for critical engagement, asking the other question, is part of the work of abolition feminism.

What Struggle Teaches

As Van Dyke's trial approached in 2018, the critical dialogues of grassroots networks sometimes crept into mainstream media outlets around questions such as: *Will prosecution of one cop really help to end racist police violence?* This question in turn spurred dialogue: *But isn't it important for people to see that the police are not above the law? If we don't prosecute, what other ways do we have to hold him, and the police, accountable?* Tensions flared about tactics for accountability, particularly between younger, queerer communities that

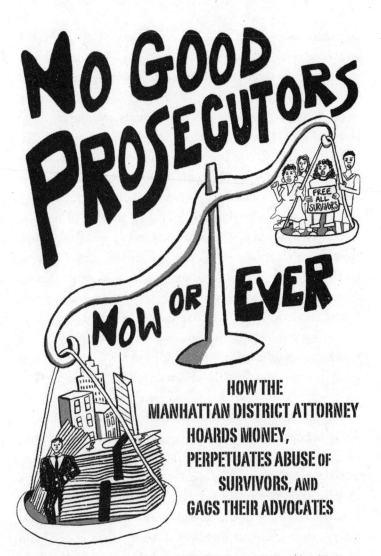

Cover by Jett George of a pamphlet distributed by Survived & Punished in 2021.

demanded changes beyond the conviction of an individual officer and older, more established civil, religious, and legal rights organizations that upheld a conviction as an important achievement.[40] Youth from Black Youth Project 100 interrupted many of then mayor of Chicago Rahm Emanuel's public events, wearing shirts emblazoned with "Fund Black Futures" and chanting "Sixteen shots and a cover up." Their "Fund Black Futures" demand worked to imagine and enact forms of accountability beyond prosecuting officers, diversifying police forces, or investing in new police trainings, and it expanded consciousness and debate about what remedies and responses might produce real safety and accountability. While some mainstream reform organizations actively pushed back, arguing that a conviction was the only way to send a clear message against police violence, it was too late: grassroots organizing had altered the terrain, insisting on the viability of radical demands.

This sense of collective power in the public struggle over police accountability led a network of immigration justice organizers to coalesce in 2018 to successfully challenge the Gang Database, a web of databases and information sharing at the county and state levels that purportedly tracked gang affiliation and other demographic information with predictive algorithms that supposedly identified those most likely to be involved in a crime. Using lawsuits, reports, direct action, and media coverage, Organized Communities Against Deportations and Mijente (in concert with other organizations) developed the #ErasetheDatabase campaign, which highlighted the scale, errors, and harmful implications of this database. As a campaign against reform, #ErasetheDatabase insisted that the only effective response to the database was to end it, and this struggle showed that a radical stance was a "winnable" demand.[41]

One distinguishing difference between the anti-police activism of previous eras and the contemporary era of Black Lives Matter is that we are not satisfied with the demand that individual police officers be prosecuted for perpetrating acts of racist violence. We also call for structural change. Neither the fact that police officer Darren Wilson was not indicted by a grand jury for the death of Mike Brown in Ferguson, Missouri, nor the indictment of police officer Brett Hankison on charges of "wanton endangerment" for the death of Breonna Taylor stalled demands to defund police. Yet the resources and the years—cumulatively centuries—many have spent trying to make the criminal legal system, including policing, accountable has not precipitated its undoing. Multiple campaigns to convict individual police of white supremacist, misogynist, and transphobic "bad acts" have not resulted in contracting the power of policing or rendering it less repressive. Civilian and other accountability watchdog organizations have had, at best, a negligible impact on reducing the violence of policing.[42] While these strategies may result in an individual police officer potentially losing their employment or being punished, the prosecution of a police officer neither undoes the system nor exposes the underlying logics and structures that perpetuate harm. Relatedly, prosecuting individual civilian men who perpetrate gender and sexual violence (or placing their names on public registries) has not reduced gender and sexual violence.[43]

Community networks and organizations struggle with how to respond to the ongoing violence of policing, just as we also collaboratively struggle to try and address gender and sexual violence outside of the arrest, prosecution, and imprisonment of individual men. We need critical debate and discussion about how to build the world we know we need. Centering the value of generative critical openness, engaged reflexivity, and the ongoing daily conditions of organizing, however, should not empty either feminism or abolition of rigor or meaning. Training police to do restorative justice work is not abolition. Hiring more women to be prison wardens is not feminist. Building a new transgender wing or pod at an immigration prison is not abolition.

These kinds of reforms bolster the budget, the scope, and the underlying logic of carceral systems. "Kinder, gentler cages" are still prisons, as Critical Resistance co-starter Rose Braz wrote in 2006 in her public response to California's proposed "gender-responsive prisons," a plan to build thirty to fifty "mini prisons" in communities across California.[44] The construction of four new smaller prisons in Manhattan, the Bronx, Brooklyn, and Queens to replace Rikers (as discussed in chapter two) deepens the very carceral problems the closure was designed to solve. None of these reforms work to dismantle, or even address, the harms that are used to buttress the carceral state, including forms of gender and sexual violence. As the state too quickly absorbs or coopts seemingly radical tools and languages, and sometimes entire organizations, in the service of legitimating state violence, abolition feminism centers a critical and generative flexibility and a culture of political education that is intimately tethered to on-the-ground social and political movements.

Sometimes the signposts between reforms that work to shrink and end our reliance on carcerality and those that deepen and grow its reach are not so obvious. Tactics are often not inherently abolitionist, rather the radical potential resides instead in the way the work unfolds and the analysis and language that form and grow as the bedrock of campaigns or strategies. Tethering short-term campaign goals to long-term struggles for paradigm shifts while ensuring that campaign participants understand the connections has always been the work of some anticapitalist queer women of color feminists. While the stakes—often our lives—do create bright lines, according to Naomi Murakawa, "Staying modal and staying intersectional are the best ways to protect ourselves from reformist improvements and move towards transformative change."[45] This politicization of methods and strategy—an attention to how organizing and labor unfolds—is important for recognizing the tensions and costs inherent in social movements: the necessity to always replace the either/or with the both/and; the need to change the rules of the game while working to ensure that people do more than simply stay alive. This both/and practice requires a willingness to inhabit contradictions, to eschew purity, and embrace the tensions and contradictions inherent in political and social movements that seek radical, systemic change. From necessity and vision, abolition feminism has always embraced at least a double practice: as Mari Matsuda reminds us, we work to ask the other question.

The Long Haul

In the fall of 2018, in a courthouse packed with uniformed officers and surrounded by protesters, Van Dyke was convicted on the lesser charge of second-degree murder and received a sentence of eighty-one months. No one was satisfied with the sentence, the first the city had handed down to a patrolman convicted of murder in almost fifty years. The Illinois Fraternal Order of Police protested the "sham trial" and a "shameful verdict."[46] Some Black community leaders were outraged by the leniency of the court when Illinois prisons were overflowing with people serving multiple lifetimes for murder rather than time meted out in months. As of this writing, the Illinois attorney general and the special prosecutor in this case are appealing to lengthen Van Dyke's sentence. As the conversation about how to hold this officer and the wider Chicago Police Department accountable continues, new starting places for struggle emerge.

Not long after the trial concluded and after the largest closure of public schools in any district in the world, Chicago accelerated its plan to build a new ninety-five-million-dollar police training academy.[47] On the heels of this verdict, when the vision and practice of safety was actively being reenvisioned and policing denaturalized, the #nocopacademy campaign and coalition emerged to challenge the building of this expensive state-of-the-art training academy. The #nocopacademy campaign produced savvy political educational materials, orchestrated creative direct actions, and did the everyday hard work of political education—on public transit, in neighborhoods, and across social media—about how the ninety-five million dollars earmarked for the new academy could be invested to really make communities—particularly Black and brown neighborhoods—safer. The *Coins, Cops, and Communities Toolkit* produced by this campaign made visible the deep asymmetries and ethical dimen-

Cover of AFSC's *Coins, Cops, and Communities Toolkit,* designed by Nicole Trinidad in 2016.

sions of a city budget. For example, Chicago's annual budget for substance abuse ($2,581,272) amounts to what Chicago spends on half a day of policing.

While the city voted to approve construction on the new police academy in late 2019, #nocopacademy expanded the political consciousness and translated abolitionist visions into a practical demand: over 120 organizations signed on and agreed that contracting the power and scope of policing is a common and achievable goal. This is an enormous win. As Chicago organizer Benji Hart noted, "The coalition lost the vote but changed the narrative on police spending."[48] The #nocopacademy campaign moved a wide range of organizations, many of which had not centered policing or abolition, to create new starting points for always emergent struggles. For example, in August 2020, when the Chicago Board of Education voted after a lengthy debate not to repeal its contract with the Chicago Police Department, an emergent campaign, #CopsoutofCPS, built on earlier conversations about abolition and labor unions to rapidly organize teach-ins over Zoom and direct actions that targeted the board of education.

Emphasizing that budgets are indications of priorities and values, the #nocopacademy and #CopsoutofCPS campaigns built on the prior work of abolition feminist organizers to disentangle public safety from policing. This work was aligned with research illustrating that the majority of calls to police are not about "crime" but about a need for support or services. As historian and scholar-activist Micol Seigel documents, police actually spend very little time dealing with the invented category of crime:

The things police do that do not have to do with "crime" could—and should—be done by other bodies: social workers, EMTs, fire fighters, traffic directors, garbage collectors, counselors, neighborhood associations, friends, and so on. That, not so incidentally, is the core of a practical, stepwise process of police abolition: begin to give nonviolent agencies, piece by piece, the tasks currently allocated to men and women in blue.[49]

This research has grounded a platform of police abolition actions nationally, including campaigns to reduce calls to 911 and to decouple or disentangle health care services from law enforcement.

Abolition feminism helped to seed the soil that made this work imaginable. This slow world of ongoing political education and coalition building can be painstaking because of the way that coalition spaces are often no one's home, as civil rights organizer and musician Bernice Johnson Reagon reminded us in 1981.[50] Detailed and relational, this necessary labor, almost never compensated or acknowledged and often falling to feminists, particularly women of color, demonstrates also that building radical community can be contagious, joyous, and "the beauty that propels the experiments in living otherwise."[51]

Beyond Success/Failure

These scattered small grassroots campaigns and organizations in a single city are only one part of the history of abolition feminism in Chicago. If known at all, they are likely viewed as disconnected, potentially even as failed projects, a laundry list of small organizations that fizzled *without passing legislation* or *achieving anything.* Other failures mount: despite a powerful campaign led in part by INCITE!, in 2017 US-Palestinian Chicago area activist Rasmea Odeh was deported.[52] Many of the small groups described in this chapter have shuttered, and are no longer in operation. Some of these campaigns involved only a handful of people. Most of their work never reached mainstream media outlets. Through one lens the list of our failures is long: an event had small turnout, the lone charismatic part-time staff member was fired, a project ran out of resources and steam and then vanished without a trace. Tensions caused the group to fracture; no one wanted to work as a collective anymore. In the context of the uprisings of 2020, most of these small groups, campaigns, and events have been forgotten or remain invisible. Not only do they deserve to be recognized as harbingers of a radical shift, but more critically their erasure weakens our ability to struggle, collectively, for the long haul.

These forms of structural erasure, a learned and organized epistemology of ignorance, is far from arbitrary: our feminist/queer/women of color histories of resistance and organizing are impoverished by intention—often lethally—and few traces remain of these powerful and often highly local campaigns that built coalitions across borders, pushing back on forms of state violence, expanding imaginations about safety and community, and seeding shifts in language and culture.[53] This erasure is made more facile by dominant metrics for success and failure created by the very systems and institutions that reproduce and naturalize racist and heteropatriarchal violence. For example, the three chapters of Critical

Resistance operating in Chicago between 2005 and 2012 tend to be forgotten because *they didn't have tangible results* for their audacious campaigns, including the 2011 "leave no child behind bars" demand to shut down the largest juvenile jail in Chicago.[54] Normative evaluative logics of success—a win is passing legislation, creating a policy or a large and permanent organization, something tangible or deliverable—are internalized, and sometimes produce shame: *What did we even do? We failed.* But as abolition feminism reminds us, while changing laws and policies might be necessary, it is never sufficient.

In this ecology of abolition feminism, the slow and urgent time of movements means that some of the most critical relationships and shifts are often unrecognizable as "wins," but these rarely acknowledged and sinewy genealogies that tether movements and campaigns across time and place continue to spark freedom. Knitted together in delicate relationships, these organizations are shifting power, building new languages, and doing the hard work to forge radical possibilities. BYP's Fund Black Futures would not have been possible without INCITE! or YWEP or the Chicago chapter of Women of All Red Nations. Chicago's Critical Resistance chapters deepened conversations about abolition that reverberated throughout the summer of 2020. Chicago Freedom School is possible because of Batey Urbano. Chicago Legal Advocacy for Incarcerated Mothers made feasible organized networks like the Prison + Neighborhood Arts / Education Project. In 2019 Chicago Community Bond Fund (CCBF) began meeting with Resilience, a large service organization in Chicago responding to sexual assault. Resilience and the CCBF met to connect the work of eliminating cash bond with the imperative to support sexual assault survivors. These tenuous linkages, rarely visible, are crucial. Yet the dominant and mainstream understanding of history, of the ecology of social and political change, is intentionally narrowed, whitewashed and straightened, and always in search of individuals and not collectives, policy/legal/legislative wins and not processes, actions, and certainly not political education or cultures that create new capaciousness for radical political consciousness.

Organized forgetting and erasure is not the only challenge. Many of these small networks fracture as a result of pressure from funders and others to expand, "scale up," "streamline," or "brand," or to provide a service rather than organize, focus on policy work not base building, elevate a single charismatic leader/director instead of a collective, network with legislators not ordinary people. Successful organizing that mobilizes people and makes effective demands on the state is sometimes coopted and absorbed because of the carceral state's ability to "beckon accommodation or conjure disappearance out of every progressive impulse."[55] The Chicago Police Department even has an Office of Restorative Justice Strategies, complete with its own Twitter feed.[56] Cooptation can mean professionalization, intimately tethered to whiteness, and the disqualification of those who have been doing this work effectively without credentials or pay and the reformation of movements and mutual aid into social service agencies and charities. Professionalization can also individuate by rejecting collectives and community, commodifying and privatizing skills, knowledges, and sometimes histories. For example, since paid employment has opened up for restorative justice

Poster illustrated by Monica Trinidad announcing a series of abolitionist events in Chicago in 2017.

practitioners and experts, many of these positions can now only be filled by someone with expensive certifications and credentials. These forms of cooptation, attention, and pressure from big philanthropy propel a narrative of failure: we tried that; it didn't work. Organized disappearance persists.

Yet these forms of cooptation are also another indication of our power: it is inevitable that mainstream political responses to movements will attempt to reject radical understandings of social problems such as the prison crisis and the gender violence pandemic. Nonetheless it is precisely our own tenacious involvement in campaigns that has pushed others in this direction. Far from being a failure, an abolition feminist ecosystem—toolkits lost on the internet, study and action groups that leaned into the former and forgot the latter, indie documentary screenings, small clusters of militant picketers, campus groups that erupt and dissipate— generated an ecology that sustained the idea that prosecuting any one police officer could not be our solution.

After sentencing, Jason Van Dyke did not immediately become one of the almost forty thousand people in the Illinois Department of Corrections: white people comprise 65 percent of the state's population and 30 percent of the state's prison population.[57] As is typical in the rare cases when police are actually convicted and sentenced, he was initially transferred to Connecticut to serve his time in a federal prison. Months after he was sentenced, his wife Tiffany announced that her husband had been assaulted in prison. She pleaded for information about his whereabouts and condition: "I don't know if he is safe at this moment or the extent of his injuries."[58] Despite her requests for information, for protection for her husband, the Bureau of Prisons refused to provide any additional information beyond acknowledging that an assault had occurred and that standard procedure required Van Dyke's segregation in the SHU, or secure housing unit. A *Chicago Tribune* headline seemed to summarize the moment: "We Can't Blame Tiffany Van Dyke for Trying, but Her Husband Is Just Another Convicted Felon."[59] Just like that, for some, Van Dyke moved from being police to felon. Perhaps he is in a prison where active organizing is underway to raise the visibility of deaths in custody; perhaps his loved ones joined the brigades of people in car caravans who procured and delivered masks and medical supplies for people inside during COVID. Perhaps.

The work in Chicago highlighted in this chapter is dynamic and ongoing. And our antecedents stretch beyond the artificial temporality of this chapter. From the journalist and anti-lynching organizer Ida B. Wells to the Communist labor and justice organizer Lucy Parsons, from the Jane Collective to Amigas Latinas, Chicago is rooted in radical change.[60] Abolition feminist mobilizations emerge from and with the strategies and analyses of previous labors. Out of necessity, people experiment and practice with the tools at hand. As the COVID-19 pandemic ebbs and deepens across the globe, the pandemic of the prison industrial complex exists alongside the pandemic of gender violence. As people strain to support loved ones, as organizers strategize alongside people surviving pandemics of COVID and criminalization and gender violence, and as groups, campaigns, and political formations continue to demand freedom from injustices that reverberate from Stateville prison to Palestine, we are energized by the passionate commitment of abolition feminists now.

Despite what some might wish—including us, on some days—there is no finish line, no firm resolute end. And yet it is hard not to read this and want concrete steps, checklists. Some guarantees. A road map. We recognize this desire. Yet—as this chapter on Chicago reminds, and as Chicago poet and educator Gwendolyn Brooks beautifully notes—*we* are our road map: "We are each other's harvest; we are each other's business; we are each other's magnitude and bond."[61] This partial Chicago archive offers a robust answer to that most important question: What do we do *now* to build abolition feminism?

EPILOGUE

How to draw a line when the work is unfolding and unfinished?

No one wanted to end this project. As organizers and writers, this caused us anxiety—sending this book to press will cement what are fluid conversations and in-process ideas. In campaigns and on-the-ground projects, a complexity of the collective "doing" or "making" is not fully documentable. Yes, we can surface interviews with participants, meeting minutes, event posters, or additional materials—often framed as evidence or ephemera. Yet the gaps and messiness and heartbreak that make a peculiar kind of sense in engagements do not necessarily translate well into written words, and their omissions can potentially read as errors in a textual project.

As scholars, even though we know histories are incomplete and contested, and we intend this book not to chronicle any "full story," we still feel pulled toward continuing to add more, to expand on examples and moments, to contextualize and to deepen as the world around us changes so rapidly: there are many places in this project that could each be a book in itself! For us, it does feel rather audacious to stop. Anywhere. Here. Particularly in a political moment when the virtual world is exploding, daily, with brilliant abolitionist and feminist tools and resources and demands. Yet, simultaneously, we know that explicitly partial genealogies are useful not only because they remind us of the fictions at the core of any chronicle that passes as complete, but also because they can interrupt a desire for reading social movements, organizations, and people hagiographically. Our labor, and the work that precedes it, is neither perfect nor finished, and neither are the movements, organizing, analysis, campaigns, and networks to come. Our snapshots aim to offer brushstrokes—a plurality of places to seek out more, an invocation to rigorously study and to engage the present, past (and future) work of collectives and campaigns—rather than fixed points of departure or dogma.

Despite our goal to not make this a comprehensive historical account but a provocation—*abolition is unthinkable without feminism and our feminism unimaginable without abolition*—we recognize many people may read this project and want templates, detailed chronologies, and definitions. Indeed, while we might be pressured to desire these at times, we understand the forms of carceral logic that compel us in these ways. There is a familiar— if often false—surety in this fixedness, and we recognize that the abolition feminism we hope to advance through this book necessitates our liberation from the tendency to get to the answer quickly.

The *Now* in the title of this book connotes our feeling of urgency and is meant to encourage thoughtful and principled action; it is not meant to suggest that there is an answer within reach at this moment. We mean: ask different questions *now*; consider alternative courses of action *now*; engage with more people *now*; complicate the analysis *now*; change our minds, apologize, recalibrate, and try again *now*. *Now* is the time for mutual aid and self-care. *Now* is the time for righteous anger and settling into the painful reality of the carnage that prisons, policing, detention—all forced confinement—have created for us. We must be reminded *right now* of how rape, battering, stalking, criminalized sex work, targeted violence toward trans people, removal of children from their families, is ruining lives. And *Now* is the time to grieve those lives lost from various pandemics, uncontrolled fires, hurricanes and earthquakes, unending war, racial capitalist exploitation, and occupations. Rather than offering the now as the end point—as in "at last"—we offer it as a critical and joyful starting point.

As we worked on the chapters—adding and refining words and examples, remembering names and events—we also learned about yet other campaigns and organizations as we solicited feedback from valued comrades. Gratitude to Rachel Caidor, Mimi Kim, and Asha Ransby-Sporn, recognition to Erin Eife, Sangeeta Ravichandran, and Mariana Green, and deep appreciation to Sara M. Benson. (We also recognize the many, many others, named and unnamed, whose thinking and practice inform this book and acknowledge the incredible labor of the Haymarket community including Anthony Arnove, Dao Tran, and Naomi Murakawa.) As we talked and wrote, around us the landscape kept changing. Over the two years we worked directly on this project, both feminism and abolition assumed new political standpoints. #MeToo/TimesUp and #DefundPolice propelled enormous and widely divergent cultural and political shifts. As the contexts transformed, the stakes and the audience for this book rose and morphed.

As *Abolition. Feminism. Now.* documents, our movements are directly responsible for this changing landscape. Our collective labors power these cultural and political shifts. Our campaigns, our demands, our organizing—posters, workshops, marches, memes, tweets, webinars, scholarship, actions, manifestos, and so much more (most produced and circulated outside of the formal economy). We are particularly energized by the proliferation of an expanding virtual world that surrounded us as we wrote this book—Zoom calls with people in prison, virtual convenings and webinars, Snapchat threads, FaceTime calls in cars and along public transit. This surge of connectivity (with access for some, not all) continues to create and strengthen rebellious inter- and intra-movement abolition feminist modalities: internationalist, interdisciplinary, and more.

We recognize and feel the impact of this growing body of work every day. Organizing meetings start in new places: for example, rather than simply accepting "carve outs" to legislation such as a post-conviction relief bill that does not apply to people with life sentences or people with convictions for sex offenses, campaigns are pushing back and refusing to sign on unless these "carve outs" are removed. Staff at anti-violence organizations are asking for, and often receiving, internal professional development that centers abolition through transformative analysis and practices. Networks are rapidly producing tools and workshops in response to the "FAQs" abolitionists frequently engage—such as the toolkit *On the Road to Freedom: An Abolitionist Assessment of Pretrial and Bail Reforms*.[1] Are any of these individual resources or actions *the* solution? No, but collectively they shape, deepen, and expand the ecosystem. And while not all these networks and tools in circulation are necessarily abolitionist or feminist, their

Networkers by Molly Costello, 2021.

invocations and practices and emergent questions/tensions—and, yes, even yearnings—seed and strengthen the ground for this growth. Revolution is not a one-time event, as Audre Lorde reminds, and these networks are making the world we need, now.[2]

As new formulations surface, others fade; networks and groups proudly identify as feminist, queer, crip, Black, and/or abolitionist. Rattled by their demands and sometimes simply their formation, dominant institutions struggle to contain and manage these movements. But yet another "diversity committee" or another "equity officer" are inevitably failed efforts to contain these insurgent demands.

Yes, in part the visible identification of networks as feminist or abolitionist could represent a shallow form of window dressing. We are not interested in abolition feminism becoming another empty signifier. But at the same time, these manifestations are also radical fissures—insurgent openings—that cannot be simply boxed up in a diversity committee or dismissed as passé. As we grapple with how to write and finish this project, mainstream news outlets are already predicting the end of the defund police movement (curiously, the complicity of mainstream feminism with gender and sexual violence—the feminist leaders and heads of feminist organizations that shielded and advised Andrew Cuomo, for example—has not propelled any death knell for #MeToo and #TimesUp[3]). But the haste with which these dominant power structures have mobilized to proclaim the end to #DefundPolice illuminates precisely the power of this demand.

Again, this is the abolition feminist imperative of the both/ and: the need to rigorously pay attention to what came before but also to move expansively and generatively and be willing to learn and unlearn. The imperative to recognize that dominant power structures will attempt—often successfully—to absorb our labor and demands, and yet we still forge new language and practices, and we work, anyway. Rather than contradictory, these tensions—painful and pleasurable—*are* the work. This book is an invitation to readers to write and organize: to create other *Aboli-*

tion. Feminism. Now. texts, films, zines, collectives, study groups, parties, and more: freedom is a constant struggle. We are one collective that has worked to push forward these linkages between abolition and feminism—and all of our work reminds us, daily, of the vibrancy of this landscape, the stakes of this work, and the imperative to learn from each other. Now.

APPENDICES

Intimate Partner Violence and State Violence
Power and Control Wheel by Monica Cosby

Intimate Partner Violence

Emotional Abuse: Makes them feel bad about themselves, calls names; makes them thing they are crazy, humiliates

Intimidation and Stalking: makes them feel afraid; damages their property; displays weapons

Coercion and Threats: carries out threats to harm; threatens to report them to other agencies

Economic Abuse: prevents them from working; makes them ask for money; takes their money

Uses Privileges: treats them like a servant; makes all big decisions; uses stereotypes against them

Minimizing, Denying, and Blaming: makes light of abuse; shifts blame for abuse saying they caused it

Isolation: controls where they go, what they do, what they read; limits work and activities

Uses Children: Makes them feel guilty about children; uses visitation to harass; threatens to take children away

State Violence

Emotional Abuse: Makes them feel bad about themselves, infantilizes them, calls names; makes them think they are crazy, humiliates

Intimidation and Stalking: shakes down their cells, strips searches, displays weapons, mandatory supervised release/parole and electronic monitoring

Coercion and Threats: threatens to call the tactical team, threatens to lose visits or programming, threatens with segregation

Economic Abuse: exploitative prison labor; extortion of commissary prices; controls how they can spend and who can give money

Uses Privileges: enforces arbitrary rules; forced to follow any and all officer rules, constant surveillance of self and property

Minimizing, Denying, and Blaming: retailiation for making grievances; says they are in prison for "their own good"

Isolation: controls who they can visit, who they can talk to by phone, reads their mail, uses solitary confinement

Uses Children: threatens to take visits away; holds DCFS programming against them; separation from children; threat of permanent separation from children

INCITE!-Critical Resistance Statement on Gender Violence and the Prison Industrial Complex (2001)

We call on social justice movements to develop strategies and analysis that address both state AND interpersonal violence, particularly violence against women. Currently, activists/movements that address state violence (such as anti-prison, anti-police brutality groups) often work in isolation from activists/movements that address domestic and sexual violence. The result is that women of color, who suffer disproportionately from both state and interpersonal violence, have become marginalized within these movements. It is critical that we develop responses to gender violence that do not depend on a sexist, racist, classist, and homophobic criminal justice system. It is also important that we develop strategies that challenge the criminal justice system and that also provide safety for survivors of sexual and domestic violence. To live violence free-lives, we must develop holistic strategies for addressing violence that speak to the intersection of all forms of oppression.

Ψ

The anti-violence movement has been critically important in breaking the silence around violence against women and providing much-needed services to survivors. However, the mainstream anti-violence movement has increasingly relied on the criminal justice system as the front-line approach toward ending violence against women of color. It is important to assess the impact of this strategy.

1) Law enforcement approaches to violence against women MAY deter some acts of violence in the short term. However, as *an overall strategy for ending violence, criminalization has not worked.* In fact, the overall impact of mandatory arrests laws for domestic violence have led to decreases in the number of battered women who kill their partners in self-defense, but they have not led to a decrease in the number of batterers who kill their partners. Thus, the law protects batterers more than it protects survivors.

2) *The criminalization approach has also brought many women into conflict with the law,* particularly women of color, poor women, lesbians, sex workers, immigrant women, women with disabilities, and other marginalized women. For instance, under mandatory arrest laws, there have been numerous incidents where police officers called to domestic incidents have arrested the woman who is being battered. Many undocumented women have reported cases of sexual and domestic violence, only to find themselves deported. A tough law and order agenda also leads to long punitive sentences for women convicted of killing their batterers. Finally, when public funding is channeled into policing and prisons, budget cuts for social programs, including women's shelters, welfare and public housing are the inevitable side effect. These cutbacks leave women less able to escape violent relationships.

3) *Prisons don't work.* Despite an exponential increase in the number of men in prisons, women are not any safer, and the rates of sexual assault and domestic violence have not decreased. In calling for greater police responses to and harsher sentences for perpetrators of gender violence, the anti-violence movement has

fueled the proliferation of prisons which now lock up more people per capita in the U.S. than any other country. During the past fifteen years, the numbers of women, especially women of color in prison has skyrocketed. Prisons also inflict violence on the growing numbers of women behind bars. Slashing, suicide, the proliferation of HIV, strip searches, medical neglect and rape of prisoners has largely been ignored by anti-violence activists. The criminal justice system, an institution of violence, domination, and control, has increased the level of violence in society.

4) *The reliance on state funding to support anti-violence programs has increased the professionalization of the anti-violence movement and alienated it from its community-organizing, social justice roots.* Such reliance has isolated the anti-violence movement from other social justice movements that seek to eradicate state violence, such that it acts in conflict rather than in collaboration with these movements.

5) *The reliance on the criminal justice system has taken power away from women's ability to organize collectively* to stop violence and has invested this power within the state. The result is that women who seek redress in the criminal justice system feel disempowered and alienated. It has also promoted an individualistic approach toward ending violence such that the only way people think they can intervene in stopping violence is to call the police. This reliance has shifted our focus from developing ways communities can collectively respond to violence.

☙

In recent years, the mainstream anti-prison movement has called important attention to the negative impact of criminalization and the build-up of the prison industrial complex. Because activists who seek to reverse the tide of mass incarceration and criminalization of poor communities and communities of color have not always centered gender and sexuality in their analysis or organizing, we have not always responded adequately to the needs of survivors of domestic and sexual violence.

1) *Prison and police accountability activists have generally organized around and conceptualized men of color as the primary victims of state violence.* Women prisoners and victims of police brutality have been made invisible by a focus on the war on our brothers and sons. It has failed to consider how women are affected as severely by state violence as men. The plight of women who are raped by INS officers or prison guards, for instance, has not received sufficient attention. In addition, women carry the burden of caring for extended family when family and community members are criminalized and where-housed. Several organizations have been established to advocate for women prisoners; however, these groups have been frequently marginalized within the mainstream anti-prison movement.

2) *The anti-prison movement has not addressed strategies for addressing the rampant forms of violence women face in their everyday lives,* including street harassment, sexual harassment at work, rape, and intimate partner abuse. Until these strategies are developed, many women will feel shortchanged by the movement. In addition, by not seeking alliances with the anti-violence movement, the anti-prison movement has sent the message that it is possible to liberate communities without seeking the well-being and safety of women.

3) *The anti-prison movement has failed to sufficiently organize around the forms of state violence faced by LGBTI communities.* LGBTI street youth and trans people in general are particularly vulnerable to police brutality and criminalization. LGBTI prisoners are denied basic human rights such as family visits from same sex partners, and same sex consensual relationships in prison are policed and punished.

4) *While prison abolitionists have correctly pointed out that rapists and serial murderers comprise a small number of the prison population, we have not answered the question of how these cases should be addressed.* The inability to answer the question is interpreted by many anti-violence activists as a lack of concern for the safety of women.

5) The various alternatives to incarceration that have been developed by anti-prison activists have *generally failed to provide a sufficient mechanism for safety and accountability for survivors of sexual and domestic violence.* These alternatives often rely on a romanticized notion of communities, which have yet to demonstrate their commitment and ability to keep women and children safe or seriously address the sexism and homophobia that is deeply embedded within them.

✤

We call on social justice movements concerned with ending violence in all its forms to:

1) *Develop community-based responses to violence that do not rely on the criminal justice system AND which have mechanisms that ensure safety and accountability for survivors of sexual and domestic*

violence. Transformative practices emerging from local communities should be documented and disseminated to promote collective responses to violence.

2) Critically assess the impact of state funding on social justice organizations and *develop alternative fundraising strategies to support these organizations.* Develop collective fundraising and organizing strategies for anti-prison and anti-violence organizations. Develop strategies and analysis that specifically target state forms of sexual violence.

3) *Make connections* between interpersonal violence, the violence inflicted by domestic state institutions (such as prisons, detention centers, mental hospitals, and child protective services), and international violence (such as war, military base prostitution, and nuclear testing).

4) *Develop an analysis and strategies to end violence that do not isolate individual acts of violence (either committed by the state or individuals) from their larger contexts.* These strategies must address how entire communities of all genders are affected in multiple ways by both state violence and interpersonal gender violence. Battered women prisoners represent an intersection of state and interpersonal violence and as such provide and opportunity for both movements to build coalitions and joint struggles.

5) *Put poor/working class women of color in the center of their analysis, organizing practices, and leadership development.* Recognize the role of economic oppression, welfare "reform," and attacks on women workers' rights in increasing women's vulnerability to all forms of violence and locate anti-violence and anti-prison activism alongside efforts to transform the capitalist economic system.

6) *Center stories of state violence committed against women of color in our organizing efforts.*

7) *Oppose legislative change that promotes prison expansion,* criminalization of poor communities and communities of color, and thus state violence against women of color, even if these changes also incorporate measure to support victims of interpersonal gender violence.

8) *Promote holistic political education* at the everyday level within our communities, specifically how sexual violence helps reproduce the colonial, racist, capitalist, heterosexist, and patriarchal society we live in as well as how state violence produces interpersonal violence within communities.

9) *Develop strategies for mobilizing against sexism and homophobia WITHIN our communities in order to keep women safe.*

10) *Challenge men of color and all men in social justice movements to take particular responsibility to address and organize around gender violence* in their communities as a primary strategy for addressing violence and colonialism. We challenge men to address how their own histories of victimization have hindered their ability to establish gender justice in their communities.

11) *Link struggles for personal transformation and healing with struggles for social justice.*

We seek to build movements that not only end violence, but that create a society based on radical freedom, mutual accountability, and passionate reciprocity. In this society, safety and security will not be premised on violence or the threat of violence; it will be based on a collective commitment to guaranteeing the survival and care of all peoples.

Supporters:

Organizations

American Friends Service Committee

Arab Women's Solidarity Association, North America

Arab Women's Solidarity Association, San Francisco Chapter

Arizona Prison Moratorium Coalition

Asian Women's Shelter

Audre Lorde Project

Black Radical Congress

Break the Chains

California Coalition for Women Prisoners

CARA / Communities Against Rape and Abuse (Seattle)

Center for Human Rights Education

Center for Immigrant Families

Center for Law and Justice

Coalition of Women from Asia and the Middle East

Colorado Progressive Alliance

Committee Against Anti-Asian Violence (New York)

Direct Action Against Refugee Exploitation (Vancouver)

East Asia-US-Puerto Rico Women's Network Against Militarism

Institute of Lesbian Studies

Justice Now

Korean American Coalition to End Domestic Abuse

Lavender Youth Recreation & Information Center (San Francisco)

Legal Services for Prisoners with Children

Minnesota Black Political Action Committee

National Coalition Against Domestic Violence

National Coalition of Anti-Violence Projects

National Network for Immigrant and Refugee Rights

Northwest Immigrant Rights Project (Seattle)

Pennsylvania Lesbian and Gay Task Force

Prison Activist Resource Center

Project South

San Francisco Women Against Rape

Shimtuh Korean Domestic Violence Program

Sista II Sista

Southwest Youth Collaborative (Chicago)

Spear and Shield Publications, Chicago

Women of All Red Nations

Women of Color Resource Center

Youth Ministries for Peace and Justice (Bronx)

Individuals

Debra M. Akuna

Gigi Alexander

Jiro Arase

Helen Arnold, Office of Sexual Misconduct Prevention & Education, Columbia University

Molefe Asante, Temple University

Rjoya K. Atu

Karen Baker, National Sexual Violence Resource Center

Rachel Baum, National Coalition of Anti-Violence Projects

Elham Bayour, Women's Empowerment Project (Gaza, Palestine)

Zoe Abigail Bermet

Eulynda Toledo-Benalli, Dine' Nation,

First Nations North & South

Diana Block, California Coalition for Women Prisoners

Marilyn Buck, Political Prisoner

Lee Carroll, National Coalition Against Domestic Violence

Emma Catague, API Women & Safety Center

Ann Caton, Young Women United

mariama changamire, Department of Communication, University of Massachusetts–Amherst

Eunice Cho, National Network for Immigrant and Refugee Rights

Sunjung Cho, KACEDA and Asian Community Mental Health Services

Christina Chu

Dorie D. Ciskowsky

Cori Couture, BAMM

Kimberle Crenshaw, UCLA Law School

Gwen D'Arcangelis

Shamita Das Dasgupta, Manavi, Inc.

Angela Y. Davis, University of California–Santa Cruz

Jason Durr, University of Hawaii School of Social Work

Michael Eric Dyson, University of Pennsylvania

Siobhan Edmondson

Michelle Erai, Santa Cruz Commission for the Prevention of Violence Against Women

Samantha Francois

Edna Frantela, National Coalition Against Domestic Violence

Loretta Frederick, Battered Women's Justice Project

Arnoldo Garcia, National Network for Immigrant and Refugee Rights

Dionne Grigsby, University of Hawaii Outreach College

Lara K. Grimm

Elizabeth Harmuth, Prison Activist Resource Center

Will Harrell, ACLU of Texas

Sarah Hoagland, Institute of Lesbian Studies

Katayoun Issari, Family Peace Center (Hawaii)

Desa Jacobsson, Anti-Violence Activist (Alaska)

Joy James, Brown University

Leialoha Jenkins

Jamie Jimenez, Northwestern Sexual Assault education Prevention Program

Dorothea Kaapana

Isabel Kang, Dorean American Coalition for Ending Domestic Abuse

Valli Kanuha, Asian Pacific Islander Institute on Domestic Violence

Mimi Kim, Asian Pacific Islander Institute on Domestic Violence

Erl Kimmich

Paul Kivel, Violence Prevention Educator

M. Carmen Lane, Anti-Violence Activist

In Hui Lee, KACEDA

Meejeon Lee, Shimtuh & KACEDA

Beckie Masaki, Asian Women's Shelter

Ann Rhee Menzie, SHIMTUH & KACEDA

Sarah Kim-Merchant, KACEDA

Patricia Manning, Alternatives to Violence Project (AVP) Volunteer

Kristin Millikan, Chicago Metropolitan Battered Women's Network

Steven Morozumi, Programs Adviser, Univ. of Oregon Multicultural Center

Soniya Munshi, Manavi

Sylvia Nam, KACEDA & KCCEB(Korean Community Center of the East Bay)

Stormy Ogden, American Indian Movement

Margo Okazawa-Rey, Mills College

Angela Naomi Paik

Ellen Pence, Praxis

Karen Porter

Trity Pourbahrami, University of Hawaii

Laura Pulido, University of Southern California

Bernadette Ramog

Matt Remle, Center for Community Justice

Monique Rhodes, Louisiana Foundation Against Sexual Assault

Lisa Richardson

Beth Richie, African American Institute on Domestic Violence

David Rider, Men Can Stop Rape

Loretta Rivera

Alissa Rojers

Clarissa Rojas, Latino Alianza Against Domestic Violence

Paula Rojas, Refuio/Refuge (New York)

Tricia Rose, University of California–Santa Cruz

Katheryn Russell-Brown, University of Maryland

Ann Russo, Women's Studies Program, DePaul University

Anuradha Sharma, Asian & Pacific Islander Institute on Domestic Violence

David Thibault Rodriguez, South West Youth Collaborative

Roxanna San Miguel

Karen Shain, Legal Services for Prisoners with Children

Proshat Shekarloo, Oakland

Anita Sinha, attorney, Northwest Immigrant Rights Project

Wendy Simonetti

Barbara Smith, founder, Kitchen Table Press

Matthea Little Smith

Natalie Sokoloff, John Jay College of Criminal Justice - CUNY

Nikki Stewart

Nan Stoops

Theresa Tevaga

Kabzuag Vaj, Hmong American Women Association

Cornel West

Janelle White, Leanne Knot Violence Against Women Consortium

Laura Whitehorn, former political prisoner

Sherry Wilson, Women of All Red Nations

Glenn Wong

Yon Soon Yoon, KACEDA

Mieko Yoshihama, University of Michigan School of Social Work

Tukufu Zuberi, Center for Africana Studies, University of Pennsylvania

Reformist Reforms vs. Abolitionist Steps to End Imprisonment

This poster is a tool to assess and understand differences between reforms that strengthen imprisonment and abolitionist steps that reduce its overall impact and grow other possibilities for wellbeing. As we work to dismantle incarceration in all its forms, we must resist common reforms that create or expand cages anywhere, including under the guise of "addressing needs" or as "updated" replacements. Jails and prisons deprive communities of resources like medical and mental health care, transportation, food, and housing. In our fights, it is critical to uplift and strategically contribute to movements led by imprisoned people, both to address pressing conditions and for abolition. In all decarceration strategies, we must utilize tactics that will improve life for those most affected and make space to build the worlds we need.

DOES THIS...	Reduce the number of people imprisoned, under surveillance, or under other forms of state control?	Reduce the reach of jails, prisons, and surveillance in our everyday lives?	Create resources and infrastructures that are steady, preventative, and accessible without police and prison guard contact?	Strengthen capacities to prevent or address harm and create processes for community accountability?
Building jails or prisons to address overcrowding or rising numbers of "new" prisoners (for example, migrants)	*NO.* If they build it, they will fill it! Building more jails and prisons creates more cages, period!	*NO.* Building more jails and prisons increases the reach of the PIC and prison and jail infrastructures. Creating more cages means building something we have to tear down later.	*NO.* Adding cages takes away state and local funding and resources that could be directed to community-led infrastructures.	*NO.* Building more prisons and jails entrenches the carceral logic of accountability. They are sites that perpetuate violence and harm.

DOES THIS...	Reduce the number of people imprisoned, etc?	Reduce the reach of jails, in our everyday lives?	Create resources without police and prison guard contact?	Strengthen capacities to prevent or address harm?
Building "closer to home," or as "nicer," "modern," "rehabilitative" alternatives to existing jails or prisons	*NO.* The history of the prison is a history of reform. New jails and prisons that are proposed as improvements on existing sites or buildings expand the arguments for and lengthen the life of imprisonment.	*NO.* There is no such thing as a "humane" cage. Construction under the pretense of addressing the harms that imprisonment reinforces the logics of using cages as a solution for social, economic, and political issues.	*NO.* Arguments for jails "closer to home" reinforce the idea that jails and police create "safety" and take away the capacity to build resources that can create well-being.	*NO.* Prisons and jails do not enable accountability. They are sites that perpetuate violence and harm.
Building jails/prisons that focus on "providing services" to address the needs of specific "populations"	*NO.* Life-affirming resources cannot be provided in spaces of imprisonment. These "services" do not decrease numbers of imprisoned people—they keep specific populations of people imprisoned.	*NO.* Building jails and prisons that lock up specific populations expands the reach of imprisonment by normalizing the idea that care can and should be coupled with policing and imprisonment.	*NO.* The argument for these jails and prisons is that they provide specialized services through policing, imprisonment, and control. Environments of control and violence cannot provide care.	*NO.* Prisons and jails do not enable accountability. They are sites that perpetuate violence and harm, and solidify oppressive social expectations around gender, sexuality, and mental health.

DOES THIS...	Reduce the number of people imprisoned, etc?	Reduce the reach of jails, in our everyday lives?	Create resources without police and prison guard contact?	Strengthen capacities to prevent or address harm?
Legislative and other efforts to single out some conviction categories as "exceptions"	*NO.* This strategy entrenches the idea that anybody "deserves" or "needs" to be locked up. Prioritizing only some people for release justifies expansion.	*NO.* By doubling-down on the "need" for some people to be locked up, these efforts strengthen and expand the reach of prisons, jails, and the PIC.	*NO.* Manufacturing divisions between imprisoned people, as more or less "dangerous," limits our ability to create real supports and resources that sustain all people.	*NO.* These efforts reinscribe the idea that some people are "risks" to society and others "deserve another chance," strengthening logics of punishment without engaging the context of how harms happen.
Use of electronic monitoring (home-arrest) and other law enforcement-led "alternatives" to jails and prisons.	*NO.* Electronic monitoring is a form of state control. It escalates the frequency of contact with the PIC for all members of a household, increasing the vulnerability of people already subject to policing and surveillance.	*NO.* Monitoring brings the prison, jail, or detention center into a person's home, turning it into a space of incarceration, which takes both a psychological and a financial toll.	*NO.* E-carceration means that regular daily movements are constantly linked to threats of arrest. This does not allow people to build and maintain community.	*NO.* E-carceration extends the violence and harm of imprisonment into people's homes and everyday lives. Nothing about electronic monitoring creates systems of accountability or healing.

DOES THIS...	Reduce the number of people imprisoned, etc?	Reduce the reach of jails, in our every-day lives?	Create resources without police and prison guard contact?	Strengthen capacities to prevent or address harm?
Public / private "partnerships" to contract services that replicate conditions of imprisonment	*NO.* These services move people from one locked facility into another facility often with similar rules and with the threat of jail or prison looming.	*NO.* This expands the reach of imprisonment, by adding to the larger system. This is particularly the case where the partner-ships replicate and expand logics and rules of jails and prisons, as opposed to intentionally challenging them.	*NO.* These programs re-quire moving through the policing and court systems to access any services that might be available there.	*NO.* Court mandated / police-run "justice" processes hold similar threats for participants as the broader PIC. They do not necessarily include meaningful processes for creating accountability or tools for preventing future harm.
Decarceration —or reducing the number of people in prisons and jails	*YES.* De-carceration takes people out of prisons and jails, and out of direct state control, with the aim of supporting people to stay outside.	*YES.* By de-prioritizing and de-legitimizing jails, prisons, and related systems we reduce the common-sense idea that they are necessary and/or "effective"	*YES.* As part of abolitionist organizing we must focus on getting people out while building strong infra-structures of support.	*YES.* When we work to diminish carceral logic, we can pair our work to-ward decarcer-ation with other ways of responding to and pre-venting harm. Investing in one will grow our capacities for the other.

DOES THIS...	Reduce the number of people imprisoned, etc?	Reduce the reach of jails, in our everyday lives?	Create resources without police and prison guard contact?	Strengthen capacities to prevent or address harm?
Shutting down existing jails and prisons and not replacing them	*YES.* By reducing the number of cages, we can reduce the number of people inside.	*YES.* When we close a jail or prison and do not replace it with other carceral systems, we chip away at the idea that cages address social, political, and economic problems.	*YES,* when we organize for it. When we fight to close jails and prisons we can open the way to defund imprisonment and invest in infrastructures locally that support and sustain people. Abolition is also a BUILDING strategy.	*YES.* Our work to close prisons and jails and keep them closed is one step toward shifting the focus to addressing and preventing harm without violence and putting resources into that work.
Rejecting government spending for jail and prison construction, renovation, expansion	*YES.* Nearly all spending projects include enhancements that support arguments for the "benefits" of incarceration.	*YES.* By rejecting spending on jails and prisons, we counter the common-sense argument that they are necessary and reduce the system's reach.	*YES.* When we reject funding for jails and prisons this can create opportunities to defund imprisonment and invest in infrastructures locally that support and sustain people.	*YES.* When we reject funding for jails and prisons this can create opportunities to defund imprisonment and invest in infrastructures locally that support and sustain people.

DOES THIS...	Reduce the number of people imprisoned, etc?	Reduce the reach of jails, in our every-day lives?	Create resources without police and prison guard contact?	Strengthen capacities to prevent or address harm?
Reducing policing and police contact in general, and "quality of life" policing, specifically	*YES.* Policing feeds impris-onment, and is an important part of sys-tems of con-trol. Reducing police contact reduces the number of people caught in the criminal legal system.	*YES.* Policing is a justifi-cation for imprisonment. By reducing police contact, the legitimacy and power of jails and prisons can be reduced.	*YES.* When we fight to reduce police contact and funding, we can free up state resources. We can orga-nize allocation to commu-nity-led infrastructures that are de-coupled from policing. We must eliminate all forms of policing from social and community services.	*YES.* Policing does not pre-vent harm, but actually causes it. Fighting to reduce polic-ing provides opportunities for communi-ties to invest in systems that prevent harm and cre-ate account-ability.

DOES THIS...	Reduce the number of people imprisoned, etc?	Reduce the reach of jails, in our everyday lives?	Create resources without police and prison guard contact?	Strengthen capacities to prevent or address harm?
Creating voluntary, accessible, community-run services and infrastructures	*YES.* Access to services that address needs people articulate for themselves can reduce vulnerability to police contact and prevent harm, while building sites for self-determination.	*YES.* Voluntary services that are community-led and -informed take power away from jails and prisons by removing the focus on imprisonment as a solution to social, economic, and political issues.	*YES.* When we create services and infrastructures that are de-coupled from policing and imprisonment we develop systems with the potential to engage with people's complex needs in consistent and trust-building ways.	*YES.* People getting their needs met in community-determined and -led ways prevents harm. By bolstering resources that address harm, without replicating harm, we create opportunities for community accountability, not punishment and isolation.

FURTHER RESOURCES

WEBSITES:

"Abolition." *Teen Vogue,* www.teenvogue.com/tag/abolition.

Alternative Justice in India, www.alternativejustice.in/about.

"Black Mamas Bail Out Action." Southerners on New Ground, https://south-ernersonnewground.org/our-work/freefromfear/black-mamas-bail-out-action.

Bronx Freedom Fund, www.thebronxfreedomfund.org.

Critical Resistance, "What Is the PIC? What Is Abolition?" http://criticalresistance.org/about/not-so-common-language.

"Embrace Supports Communities of Color." Embrace, https://www.docu-mentcloud.org/documents/20398151-embrace-statement-on-support-ing-communities-of-color.

Erase the Database, http://erasethedatabase.com.

Flat Out, http://www.flatout.org.au.

INCITE! Women, Gender-Nonconforming, and Trans People of Color Against Violence, https://incite-national.org.

Rasmea Defense Committee, http://justice4rasmea.org.

She Safe, We Safe, https://www.shesafewesafe.org.

Sisters Inside, https://sistersinside.com.au.

"Sisters Uncut Stands in Solidary with the Wet'suwet'en." Sisters Uncut, February 20, 2020, https://www.sistersuncut.org/2020/02/20/sisters-un-cut-stands-in-solidarity-with-the-wetsuweten.

Survivors for Divestment, http://www.defendsurvivorsnow.org/survivors-for-divestment.

BOOKS AND ARTICLES

Alexander, Elizabeth. "The Trayvon Generation." *New Yorker,* June 15, 2020.

Alexander, Michelle. *The New Jim Crow: Mass Incarceration in the Age of Color-blindness.* New York: New Press, 2010.

Allen, Robert. *Black Awakening in Capitalist America.* New York: Doubleday, 1969.

American Friends Service Committee Working Party. *Struggle for Justice: A Report on Crime and Punishment in America.* New York: Hill and Wang, 1971.

Anzaldúa, Gloria. *Borderlands/La Frontera: The New Mestiza.* San Francisco: Aunt Lute, 1987.

Baker, Ella and Marvel Cooke. "Bronx Slave Market." *The Crisis* (November 1935): 330–32.

Bassichis, Morgan, Alexander Lee, and Dean Spade. "Building an Abolitionist Trans & Queer Movement with Everything We've Got." In *Captive Genders: Trans Embodiment and the Prison Industrial Complex.* Oakland: AK Press, 2011.

Beal, Fran. "Double Jeopardy: To Be Black and Female." In *Sisterhood Is Powerful,* edited by Robin Morgan. New York: Vintage, 1970.

Beal, Fran. "Double Jeopardy: To Be Black and Female." In *The Black Woman: An Anthology,* edited by Toni Cade Bambara. New York: New American Library Publishers, 1970.

Ben-Moshe, Liat. *Decarcerating Disability: Deinstitutionalization and Prison Abolition.* Minneapolis: University of Minnesota Press, 2020.

Bennett, Hans. "Organizing to Abolish the Prison-Industrial Complex." *Dissident Voice.* July 11, 2008. https://dissidentvoice.org/2008/07/organizing-to-abolish-the-prison-industrial-complex.

Berger, Dan and Emily K. Hobson. *Remaking Radicalism: A Grassroots Documentary Reader of the United States, 1973–2001.* Athens: University of Georgia Press, 2020.

Bernstein, Elizabeth. "The Sexual Politics of the 'New Abolitionism.'" *differences* 18, no. 3 (2007): 128–51.

Bhattacharjee, Anannya. "Whose Safety? Women of Color and the Violence of Law Enforcement." Philadelphia: American Friends Service Committee, Committee on Women, Population, and the Environment, 2001, https://www.afsc.org/sites/default/files/documents/whose%20safety.pdf.

Biasco, Paul and Mitchell Armentrout. "Police Union Blasts 'Sham Trial and Shameful' Van Dyke Guilty Verdict." *Chicago Sun Times.* October 5, 2018, https://chicago.suntimes.com/2018/10/5/18460941/police-union-blasts-sham-trial-and-shameful-van-dyke-guilty-verdict.

Bindel, Julie. *The Pimping of Prostitution: Abolishing the Sex Work Myth.* London: Palgrave, 2017.

Braden, Anne. "Free Thomas Wansley: A Letter to White Southern Women." Louisville: SCEF Press, 1972. At https://newsreel.org/guides/Anne-Braden-A-Letter-to-White-Southern-Women.pdf.

Braz, Rose. "Kinder, Gentler, Gender Responsive Cages: Prison Expansion Is Not Prison Reform." *Women, Girls & Criminal Justice* (October/November 2006): 87–91.

brown, adrienne maree. *Emergent Strategies: Shaping Change, Changing Worlds.* Chico, CA: AK Press, 2017.

Brown, Elsa Barkley. "'What Has Happened Here': The Politics of Difference in Women's History and Feminist Politics." *Feminist Studies* 18, no. 2 (Summer 1992): 295–312.

Byrne, John. "Mayor Rahm Emanuel Announces Next Step in Police Academy Project, a Plan That Continues to Draw Criticism." *Chicago Tribune.* November 16, 2018. https://www.chicagotribune.com/politics/ct-met-rahm-emanuel-police-academy-20181116-story.html.

Camp, Jordan T. and Christina Heatherton. "How Liberals Legitimate Broken Windows: An Interview with Naomi Murakawa." In *Policing the Planet: Why the Policing Crisis Led to Black Lives Matter,* edited by Jordan T. Camp and Christina Heatherton, 227–36. New York: Verso, 2016.

Chammah, Maurice. "Do You Age Faster in Prison?" The Marshall Project. August 24, 2015. https://www.themarshallproject.org/2015/08/24/do-you-age-faster-in-prison.

Chen, Ching-In, Jai Dulani, and Leah Lakshmi Piepzna-Samarasinha. *The Revolution Starts at Home: Confronting Intimate Violence Within Activist Communities*. Brooklyn, NY: South End Press, 2016.

Cherone, Heather. "Pritzker Unveils Plan to 'Transform' Juvenile Justice in Illinois by Closing Large Facilities." WTTW News. July 31, 2020. https://news.wttw.com/2020/07/31/pritzker-unveils-plan-transform-juvenile-justice-illinois-closing-large-facilities.

Combahee River Collective. "Combahee River Collective Statement." In *Let Nobody Turn Us Around: Voices of Resistance, Reform, and Renewal*, edited by Manning Marable and Leith Mullings, 501–506. New York: Rowman and Littlefield, 2000.

Committee on Domestic Violence and Incarcerated Women. "Battered Women and Criminal Justice: A Report of the Committee on Domestic Violence and Incarcerated Women." June 1987. https://www.ojp.gov/pdffiles1/Digitization/107516NCJRS.pdf.

Community Organizing and Family Issues. "Parent-to-Parent Guide: Restorative Justice in Chicago Public Schools." Power-Pac Elementary Justice Campaign. December 2015, https://www.cofionline.org/COFIwp-content/uplaods/2016/06/COFI-P2P-guide-update-2015.pdf.

Congressional Research Service. "The Violence Against Women Act (VAWA): Historical Overview, Funding, and Reauthorization." April 23, 2019. https://fas.org/sgp/crs/misc/R45410.pdf.

Cordoso, Tom and Molly Hayes. "Canadian Cities' Police Spending Ranges from One-10th to Nearly a Third of Total Budgets, Globe Analysis Finds." *Globe and Mail*. August 16, 2020. https://www.theglobeandmail.com/canada/article-canadian-cities-police-spending-ranges-from-one-10th-to-nearly-a/?fbclid=IwAR01RaMqqKluvsXm-D1XJjBHnAbOHTxKDa6AsUhVB4isjKiuP6NAXJzPD0hI.

Creative Interventions, "Creative Interventions Toolkit: A Practical Guide to Stop Interpersonal Violence." 2021. https://www.creative-interventions.

org/toolkit.

Crenshaw, Kimberlé. "Mapping the Margins: Intersectionality, Identity Politics, and Violence against Women of Color." *Stanford Law Review* 43, no. 6 (July 1991): 1241–99.

Critical Resistance Publications Collective. "Special Edition: Critical Resistance to the Prison-Industrial Complex." *Social Justice* 27, no. 3 (2000).

Davis, Angela Y. "Masked Racism: Reflections on the Prison Industrial Complex." Colorlines. September 10, 1998.

———. *Freedom Is a Constant Struggle: Ferguson, Palestine, and the Foundations of a Movement.* Chicago: Haymarket Books, 2015.

Davis, Angela and Gina Dent. "Prison as a Border: A Conversation on Gender, Globalization, and Punishment." *Signs* 26, no. 4 "Globalization and Gender" (Summer 2001): 1235–41.

Davis, Mike. "Hell Factories in the Field: A Prison-Industrial Complex." *Nation.* February 20, 1995.

Dixon, Ejeris and Leah Lakshmi Piepzna-Samarasinha. *Beyond Survival: Strategies and Stories from the Transformative Justice Movement.* Chico, CA: AK Press, 2020.

DLA Piper and Association for the Prevention of Torture. "A Global Analysis of Prisoner Releases in Response to COVID-19." DLAPiper.com. December 2020. www.dlapiper.com/~/media/files/insights/publications/2021/03/dla-piper-prison-population-during-covid-19.pdf?la=en&hash=F5C1EB-BA0D3D86BDDA58FAC87DB9EF3CAE3815DF.

Duane, Anna Mae and Erica Meiners. "Working Analogies: Slavery Now and Then." In *Fighting Modern Slavery and Human Trafficking: History and Contemporary Policy,* edited by Jessica Pliley, Genevieve LaBaron, and David W. Blight (Cambridge, UK: Cambridge University Press, 2021).

Du Bois, W. E. B. *Black Reconstruction in America: An Essay Toward a History of the Part Which Black Folk Played in the Attempt to Reconstruct Democracy in America, 1860–1880.* New York: The Free Press, 1998 [1935].

Ellis, Eddie. "An Open Letter to Our Friends on the Question of Language." Center for Nuleadership on Urban Solutions. 2007. https://cmjcenter.org/wp-content/uploads/2017/07/CNUS-AppropriateLanguage.pdf.

Faith, Karlene. *Unruly Women: The Politics of Confinement & Resistance.* New

York: Seven Stories Press, 2011 [1993].

Gilmore, Ruth Wilson. *Golden Gulag: Prisons, Surplus, Crisis, and Opposition in Globalizing California.* Berkeley: University of California Press, 2007.

Glanton, Dahleen. "We can't blame Tiffany Van Dyke for trying, but Her Husband Is Just Another Convicted Felon." *Chicago Tribune.* February 16, 2019. https://www.chicagotribune.com/columns/dahleen-glanton/ct-met-dahleen-glanton-jason-van-dyke-beating-20190215-story.html.

Goldstein, Leslie F. "Early Feminist Themes in French Utopian Socialism: The Saint-Simonians and Fourier." *Journal of the History of Ideas* 43, no. 1 (January 1982): 91–108.

Gorz, André. *Strategy for Labor: A Radical Proposal.* Boston: Beacon, 1967.

Grant, Melissa Gira. "An Anti-Rape Movement Without Police." *New Republic.* October 20, 2020. https://newrepublic.com/article/159850/anti-rape-movement-without-police.

Gustafson, Kaaryn S. *Cheating Welfare: Public Assistance and the Criminalization of Poverty.* New York: New York University Press, 2011.

Gwinn, Casey and Gael Strack. "Another Perspective on 'The Moment of Truth.'" *Domestic Violence Report,* 26, no. 2. December/January 2021.

Haley, Sarah. *No Mercy Here: Gender, Punishment and Jim Crow Modernity.* Chapel Hill: University of North Carolina Press, 2016.

Hall, Stuart, et al. *Policing the Crisis: Mugging, the State, and Law and Order.* London: Macmillan, 1978.

Hart, Benji. "Misogyny on the Mag Mile: A Turning Point." Radical Faggot. December 2, 2015. https://radfag.com/2015/12/02/misogyny-on-the-mag-mile-a-turning-point/.

———. "How #NoCopAcademy Shook the Machine." *Chicago Reader.* April 26, 2019. https://www.chicagoreader.com/chicago/how-nocopacademy-shook-the-machine/Content?oid=69862164.

Hartman, Saidiya. *Wayward Lives, Beautiful Experiments: Intimate Histories of Riotous Black Girls, Troublesome Women, and Queer Radicals.* New York: Norton, 2019.

Harvey, David. *The Limits to Capital.* London: Verso, 2018.

INCITE! Women of Color Against Violence. *The Revolution Will Not Be Funded: Beyond the Non-Profit Industrial Complex.* Durham, NC: Duke University

Press, 2017.

"Inside Prison Amid Coronavirus Pandemic: Incarcerated Journalist Says Millions Behind Bars at Risk." Interview with Juan Moreno Haines. Democracy Now! March 17, 2020. https://www.democracynow.org/2020/3/17/coronavirus_prisons_san_quentin.

Jackson, Esther Cooper. "The Negro Domestic Worker in Relation to Trade Unionism." Master's thesis. Fisk University, 1940. Republished in Viewpoint Magazine. October 31, 2015. https://viewpointmag.com/2015/10/31/the-negro-woman-domestic-worker-in-relation-to-trade-unionism-1940.

Jones, Claudia. "An End to the Neglect of the Problems of the Negro Woman!" *Political Affairs* 28, no. 6 (1949): 51–67.

Kaba, Mariame and Shira Hassan. *Fumbling Towards Repair: Workbook for Community Accountability Facilitators.* Project NIA, 2019.

Kaepernick, Colin. *Abolition for the People: The Movement for a Future Without Policing & Prisons.* Kaepernick Publishing, 2021.

Karp, Sarah. "Black Teachers Hit Harder by CPS Layoffs." Better Government Association. September 2, 2015. https://www.bettergov.org/news/black-teachers-hit-harder-by-cps-layoffs.

Kilgore, James. "Repackaging Mass Incarceration." Counterpunch. June 6, 2014. https://www.counterpunch.org/2014/06/06/repackaging-mass-incarceration.

Kim, Alice. "Breaking Walls: Lessons from Chicago." In T*he Long Term: Resisting Life Sentences, Working Toward Freedom*, edited by Alice Kim, Erica R. Meiners, Audrey Petty, Jill Petty, Beth E. Richie, and Sarah Ross. Chicago: Haymarket Books, 2018.

Kim, Mimi E. "Anti-Carceral Feminism: The Contradictions of Progress and the Possibilities of Counter-Hegemonic Struggle." *Affilia* 35, no. 3 (2020): 309–26.

———. "The Carceral Creep: Gender-Based Violence, Race and the Expansion of the Punitive State, 1973–1983." *Social Problems* 67, no. 2 (2020): 251–69.

———. "VAWA @ 20: The Mainstreaming of the Criminalization Critique: Reflections on VAWA 20 Years Later." *City University of New York Law Review*

18, no. 1 (2014): 52–57.

King, Deborah K. "Multiple Jeopardy, Multiple Consciousness: The Context of a Black Feminist Ideology." *Signs* 14, no. 1 (Autumn 1988): 42–72.

Knopp, Fay Honey. "Radical Feminism and Abolition." *Peace Review* 6, no. 2 (1994): 203–208.

Lancaster, Roger. "How to End Mass Incarceration." *Jacobin*, August 18, 2017. https://jacobinmag.com/2017/08/mass-incarceration-prison -abolition-policing.

Levenstein, Lisa. *They Didn't See Us Coming: The Hidden History of Feminism in the Nineties.* New York: Basic Books, 2020.

Lopez, German. "The First Step Act, Explained." Vox. February 5, 2019. At https://www.vox.com/future-perfect/2018/12/18/18140973/state-of-the-union-trump-first-step-act-criminal-justice-reform.

Lorde, Audre. *Zami: A New Spelling of My Name.* Berkeley, CA: Crossing Press, 1982.

———. "Age, Race, Class and Sex: Women Redefining Difference." In *Sister Outsider: Essays and Speeches*, 114–23. Berkeley, CA: Crossing Press, 1984.

———. "The Uses of Anger: Women Responding to Racism." *In Sister Outsider: Essays and Speeches*, 124–33. Berkeley, CA: Crossing Press, 1984.

Lowrey, Annie. "Her Only Crime Was Helping Her Kids." *Atlantic.* September 13, 2019. https://www.theatlantic.com/ideas/archive/2019/09/her-only-crime-was-helping-her-kid/597979/.

Mansfield, Maureen. "What Is Abolition Feminism, and Why Does It Matter?" IPPR Progressive Review. June 13, 2018. https://www.ippr.org /juncture-item/what-is-abolitionist-feminism-and-why-does-it-matter.

Mathiesen, Thomas. *The Politics of Abolition.* London: Martin Robertson and Company, 1974.

Matsuda, Mari. "Beside My Sister, Facing the Enemy: Legal Theory Out of Coalition." *Stanford Law Review* 43, no. 6 (1991): 1183–92.

———. "Crime and Punishment." *Ms. Magazine* (November/December 1994): 86–88.

Melamed, Jodi. "Racial Capitalism." *Critical Ethnic Studies* 1, no. 1 (2015): 76–85.

Mills, Charles. *The Racial Contract.* Ithaca, NY: Cornell University Press, 1997.

"Moment of Truth." June 2020. https://www.violencefreecolorado.org/wp-content/uploads/2020/07/Moment-of-Truth.pdf.

Moser, Laura."The Awkward Radicalization of the Chicago Teacher's Union." Slate. April 7, 2016. https://slate.com/human-interest/2016/04/chicago-teachers-union-is-going-through-an-awkward-radicalization.html.

National Center for Transgender Equality. "The Report of the 2015 US Transgender Survey Executive Summary," December 2016. https://transequality.org/sites/default/files/docs/usts/USTS-Executive-Summary-Dec17.pdf.

Nestle, Joan. "Women's House of Detention, 1931–1974." Outhistory. 2008. https://outhistory.org/exhibits/show/historical-musings/womens-house-of-detention.

Pacheco, Antonio. "Interrogating the Impacts of NYC's Rikers Jail Replacement Plan." Archinect News. December 12, 2019. https://archinect.com/news/article/150174335/interrogating-the-impacts-of-nyc-s-rikers-jail-replacement-plan.

Patterson, Orlando. *Slavery and Social Death: A Comparative Study*. Cambridge, MA: Harvard University Press, 1982.

People Against Prisons Aotearoa in Aoteroa/New Zealand. "Transformative Justice Workshop: Practical Ways of Solving Interpersonal Harm and Conflict in our Communities." https://papa-site-assets.ams3.cdn.digitaloceanspaces.com/publications/transformative-justice-workshop-v2.pdf.

Perkinson, Robert. *Texas Tough: The Rise of America's Prison Empire*. New York: Henry Holt, 2010.

Piercy, Marge. "To Be of Use." From *Circles in the Water: Selected Poems of Marge Piercy*. New York: Alfred A. Knopf. (1982), https://www.poetryfoundation.org/poems/57673/to-be-of-use.

Prison Policy Institute. "The Most Significant Criminal Justice Policy Changes from the COVID-19 Pandemic." May 18, 2021. https://www.prisonpolicy.org/virus/virusresponse.html.

Prison Research Education Action Project. *Instead of Prisons: A Handbook for Abolitionists*. Syracuse: Prison Research Education Action Project, 1976.

Quinn, Therese and Erica R. Meiners. "Good Cop? Bad Cop? No Cop! Queer Resistance to Policing." *Windy City Times*. July 29, 2015.

Quinnell, Kenneth. "Get to Know AFL-CIO's Affiliates: International Union

of Police Associations." AFL-CIO. September 23, 2019. https://aflcio.
org/2019/9/23/get-know-afl-cios-affiliates-international-union
-police-associations.

Reagon, Bernice Johnson. "Coalition Politics: Turning the Century." In *Home
Girls: A Black Feminist Anthology*, edited by Barbara Smith, 343–56. New
York: Kitchen Table Press, 1983.

"Reimagining Justice in South Africa Beyond Policing." Produced by Cops Are
Flops. https://drive.google.com/file/d/1krNcg_saPFABqjuFkQvtVK-
UpIjivd8Es/view?fbclid=IwAR2ve10x0CSPi9sipQdXyD2vdYHI_lYzu-
FYMQ0PTHX26m4WfR6sz8e0nT2I.

Richie, Beth E. *Arrested Justice: Black Women, Violence, and America's Prison
Nation*. New York: New York University Press, 2016.

———. *Compelled to Crime: The Gender Entrapment of Battered Black Women*.
New York: Routledge, 1996.

Richie, Beth, Dylan Rodríguez, Mariame Kaba, Melissa Burch, Rachel Herzing,
and Shana Agid. "Problems with Community Control of Police and Proposals for Alternatives," https://static1.squarespace.com/static
/5ee39ec764dbd7179cf1243c/t/6008c586b43eee58a4c4b73e
/1611187590375/Problems+with+Community+Control.pdf.

Ritchie, Andrea. *Invisible No More: Police Violence Against Black Women and
Women of Color*. Boston: Beacon Press, 2017.

Ritchie, Andrea J. and Joey L. Mogul. "In the Shadows of the War on Terror:
Persistent Police Brutality and Abuse of People of Color in the United
States: A Report Prepared for the United Nations Committee on the Elimination of Racial Discrimination." *DePaul Journal for Social Justice* 1, no. 2
(2008): 175–250.

Roberts, Dorothy. "Abolishing Policing Also Means Abolishing Family
Regulation." The Imprint. June 16, 2020. https://imprintnews.org/
child-welfare-2/abolishing-policing-also-means-abolishing-family reg-
ulation/44480?fbclid=IwAR1vfOAeWs9vZ1ZhAfCCyC5WPoSjPMX-
bQ6g8vJkV9x7rPklfBQ-AgD1WIX4.

———. "'Abolition Is the Only Answer': A Conversation with Dorothy Roberts."
Rise. October 20, 2020. https://www.risemagazine.org/2020/10/conver-
sation-with-dorothy-roberts.

————.*Killing the Black Body: Race, Reproduction, and the Meaning of Liberty.* New York: Vintage, 1997.

Robinson, Cedric J. *Black Marxism: The Making of the Black Radical Tradition.* Durham, NC: University of North Carolina Press, 1983.

Romano, Aja. "A New Law Intended to Curb Sex Trafficking Threatens the Future of the Internet as We Know It." Vox. July 2, 2018. https://www.vox.com/culture/2018/4/13/17172762/fosta-sesta-backpage-230 -internet-freedom.

Russo, Ann. *Feminist Accountability: Disrupting Violence and Transforming Power.* New York University Press, 2018.

Russo, Ann and Melissa Spatz. "Communities Engaged in Resisting Violence." Women & Girls Collective Action Network. 2008. https://comm-org.wisc.edu/papers2008/russo.htm#What_You_Can_Do!.

"Santa Cruz Women's Prison Project Newsletter, February 1974." Freedom Archives. http://freedomarchives.org/Documents/Finder/DOC70_scans/70.SCWPP.Newsletter.Feb1974.pdf.

Schechter, Susan. *Women and Male Violence: The Visions and Struggles of the Battered Women's Movement.* Boston: South End Press, 1982.

Sedgwick, Eve Kosofsky. *Epistemology of the Closet.* Cambridge, MA: Harvard University Press, 1990.

Sharpe, Cristina. *In the Wake: On Blackness and Being.* Durham, NC: Duke University Press, 2016.

Seigel, Micol. *Violence Work: State Power and the Limits of Police.* Durham, NC: Duke University Press, 2018.

Simeone-Casas, Jenny and Sarah Conway. "Grandmothers of Chicago's Restorative Justice Movement." City Bureau. January 3, 2018. https://www.citybureau.org/stories/2018/3/1/grandmothers-of-chicagos -restorative-justice-movement.

Simmons, Tommy. "Law Enforcement Groups Withdraw Support of Idaho Coalition Over Letter Calling for Racial Justice." *Idaho State Journal,* October 21, 2020.

Smith, Barbara, ed. *Home Girls: A Black Feminist Anthology.* New York: Kitchen Table: Women of Color Press, 1983.

Stanley, Eric and Nat Smith, eds. *Captive Genders: Trans Embodiment and the*

Prison Industrial Complex. Oakland, CA: AK Press, 2011.

Sudbury, Julia (now Chinyere Oparah), ed. *Global Lockdown: Race, Gender, and the Prison-Industrial Complex*. London: Routledge, 2005.

Swanson, Lorraine. "Tiffany Van Dyke: 'I Can't Bury My Husband.'" Patch.com. February 14, 2019. https://patch.com/illinois/chicago/wife-says-she-was-kept-dark-jason-van-dyke-s-beating.

Taylor, Flint. "How Activists Won Reparations for the Survivors of Chicago Police Department Torture." *In These Times*. June 26, 2015. http://inthese-times.com/article/18118/jon-burge-torture-reparations.

Taylor, Keeanga-Yamahtta, ed. *How We Get Free: Black Feminism and the Comba-hee River Collective*. Chicago: Haymarket Books, 2017.

Thompson, Heather. *Blood in the Water: The Attica Prison Uprising of 1971 and Its Legacy*. New York: Pantheon 2016.

Tung, Liz. "FOSTA-SESTA Was Supposed to Thwart Sex Trafficking. Instead, It's Sparked a Movement." PBS. July 10, 2020. https://whyy.org/segments/fosta-sesta-was-supposed-to-thwart-sex-trafficking-instead-its-sparked-a-movement.

Venteicher, Wes. "'No Evident Justification' for California Prison Guard Raises in Contract, Analyst Warns." *Sacramento Bee*. June 17, 2019, https://www.sacbee.com/news/politics-government/the-state-worker/arti-cle231649048.html.

Violent Crime Control and Law Enforcement Act of 1994. US Department of Justice Fact Sheet. https://www.ncjrs.gov/txtfiles/billfs.txt.

Vitale, Alex. *The End of Policing*. London: Verso, 2017.

Wahlquist, Calla. "Crowdfunding Campaign to Free Indigenous Women 'Shocked' by WA Response." *Guardian*. January 22, 2019. https://www.theguardian.com/australia-news/2019/jan/23/crowdfunding-campaign-to-free-indigenous-women-shocked-by-wa-government-response.

Walia, Harsha. *Undoing Border Imperialism*. Oakland, CA: AK Press, 2013.

Walker, Darren. "In Defense of Nuance." Ford Foundation. September 19, 2019. https://www.fordfoundation.org/ideas/equals-change-blog/posts/in-de-fense-of-nuance.

Wang, Jackie. *Carceral Capitalism*. Cambridge, MA: MIT Press, 2018.

"We Charge Genocide," Police Violence Against Chicago's Youth of Color: A

Report Prepared for the United Nations Committee Against Torture."
    September 2014. http://report.wechargegenocide.org.

Weiss, Robert P., ed. "Special Edition: Attica: 1971–1991—A Commemorative
    Issue." *Social Justice* 18, no. 3 (1991).

Williams, Kristian. *Our Enemies in Blue: Police and Power in America*. Oakland,
    CA: AK Press, 2015.

"Women's House of Detention Protects the First Offenders." *New York Times*.
    March 8, 1931.

Woodard, Stephanie. "The Police Killings No One Is Talking About." *In These
    Times*. October 17, 2016. https://inthesetimes.com/features/native_amer-
    ican_police_killings_native_lives_matter.html.

Wright, Paul. "Slaves of the State." In *The Celling of America: An Inside Look at
    the U.S. Prison Industry*. Monroe, ME: Common Courage, 1998: 102–6.

NOTES

Preface

1. What was then called INCITE! Women of Color Against Violence is now called INCITE! Women, Gender Non-Conforming, and Trans People of Color Against Violence. See https://incite-national.org.
2. We note, as we write, that Mills College, with a majority women-of-color and LGBTQ student population, recently announced its closing and shortly afterwards, its possible merger with Northeastern University. With its significance for so many progressive movements, the non-viability of an independent future for this campus in the heart of the city of Oakland is a casualty with multiple causes.
3. "Abolition," *Teen Vogue*, at https://www.teenvogue.com/tag/abolition.
4. See, for example, Angela Y. Davis's *Freedom Is a Constant Struggle: Ferguson, Palestine, and the Foundations of a Movement* (Chicago: Haymarket Books, 2016).
5. See, for example, Barbara Smith's (1983) *Home Girls: A Black Feminist Anthology* (New York: Kitchen Table: Women of Color Press); the Combahee River Collective's "Combahee River Collective Statement," in *Let Nobody Turn Us Around: Voices of Resistance, Reform, and Renewal*, edited by Manning Marable and Leith Mullings (New York: Rowman and Littlefield, 2000), 501–506; and Keeanga-Yamahtta Taylor's edited volume, *How We Get Free: Black Feminism and the Combahee River Collective* (Chicago: Haymarket Books, 2017).
6. Elsa Barkley Brown, "'What Has Happened Here': The Politics of Difference in Women's History and Feminist Politics," *Feminist Studies* 18, no. 2 (Summer 1992): 295–312.

Introduction

1. Mari Matsuda, "Beside My Sister, Facing the Enemy: Legal Theory Out of Coalition," *Stanford Law Review* 43, no. 6 (1991): 1183, 1189.

2. Fran Beal's "Double Jeopardy: To Be Black and Female" was initially published as a pamphlet and later revised and published in Toni Cade's *The Black Woman: An Anthology* (New York: New American Library Publishers, 1970). *Triple Jeopardy* was the title of the newspaper of the Third World Women's Alliance, and "Racism, Sexism, Imperialism" was on its masthead. See also Deborah K. King, "Multiple Jeopardy, Multiple Consciousness: The Context of a Black Feminist Ideology," *Signs* 14, no. 1 (Autumn 1988): 42–72 and Kimberlé Crenshaw, "Mapping the Margins: Intersectionality, Identity Politics, and Violence against Women of Color," *Stanford Law Review* 43, no. 6 (July 1991): 1241–99.

3. In Dean Spade's *Mutual Aid: Building Solidarity during This Crisis (and the Next)* (London: Verso, 2020), Spade suggests that "mutual aid is one term used to describe collective coordination to meet each other's needs, usually stemming from an awareness that the systems we have in place are not going to meet them."

4. People Against Prisons Aotearoa in Aotearoa/New Zealand, "Transformative Justice Workshop: Practical Ways of Solving Interpersonal Harm and Conflict in our Communities," at https://papa-site-assets.ams3.cdn.digita-loceanspaces.com/publications/transformative-justice-workshop-v2.pdf.

5. Mariame Kaba and Shira Hassan, *Fumbling Towards Repair: Workbook for Community Accountability Facilitators* (Project NIA, 2019).

6. Ejeris Dixon and Leah Lakshmi Piepzna-Samarasinha, *Beyond Survival: Strategies and Stories from the Transformative Justice Movement* (Chico, CA: AK Press, 2020) and Ching-In Chen, Jai Dulani, and Leah Lakshmi Piepzna-Samarasinha, *The Revolution Starts at Home: Confronting Intimate Violence Within Activist Communities* (Brooklyn, NY: South End Press, 2016).

7. See also *Abolition for the People: The Movement for a Future without Policing & Prisons*, ed. Colin Kaepernick (Kaepernick Publishing, 2021).

8. Nicole Fleetwood, *Marking Time: Art in the Age of Mass Incarceration*

(Cambridge: Harvard University Press, 2020).

9. For more on the Fund Black Futures demand of organizations such as the Black Youth Project 100, see David Turner, "#ResistCapitalism to #Fund-BlackFutures: Black Youth, Political Economy, and the 21st Century Black Radical Imagination" in Abolition Journal (12/8/2016), https://abolition-journal.org/resistcapitalism-to-fundblackfutures.

10. See Papel Machete's performance: https://www.youtube.com/watch?v=qtAPHtG0hLQ.

11. See Avery F. Gordon's work, especially *The Hawthorne Archive: Letters from the Utopian Margins* (New York: Fordham University Press, 2013).

12. On "evangelical zeal," see Roger Lancaster, "How to End Mass Incarceration," *Jacobin*, August 18, 2017, https://jacobinmag.com/2017/08/mass-incarceration-prison-abolition-policing. On "extremism," see Darren Walker, "In Defense of Nuance," Ford Foundation September 19, 2019, https://www.fordfoundation.org/ideas/equals-change-blog/posts/in-defense-of-nuance.

13. Harsha Walia, *Undoing Border Imperialism* (Chico, CA: AK Press, 2013).

14. Hans Bennett, "Organizing to Abolish the Prison-Industrial Complex," July 11, 2008, Dissident Voice, https://dissidentvoice.org/2008/07/organizing-to-abolish-the-prison-industrial-complex.

15. For a critique of hate crimes legislation, see Morgan Bassichis, Alexander Lee, and Dean Spade, "Building an Abolitionist Trans & Queer Movement with Everything We've Got," in *Captive Genders: Trans Embodiment and the Prison Industrial Complex*, edited by Eric Stanley and Nat Smith (Oakland, CA: AK Press, 2011).

16. *Reimagining Justice in South Africa Beyond Policing*, produced by CopsAreFlops, https://drive.google.com/file/d/1krNcg_saPFABq-juFkQvtVKUpIjivd8Es/view?fbclid=IwAR2ve10x0CSPi9sipQdXyD-2vdYHI_IYzuFYMQ0PTHX26m4WfR6sz8e0nT2I. CopsAreFlops is a youth-led initiative dedicated to imagining and working towards a South African justice system beyond policing and incarceration. CopsAreFlops can be found on Instagram, Facebook, and Twitter:@copsareflops.

17. Theorists like Jodi Melamed, building from Cedric Robinson's work in *Black Marxism: The Making of the Black Radical Tradition* (Durham: Uni-

versity of North Carolina Press, 1983), write that capitalism is always *racial capitalism*: "Capital can only be capital when it is accumulating, and it can only accumulate by producing and moving through relations of severe inequality among human groups." Jodi Melamed, "Racial Capitalism," *Critical Ethnic Studies* 1, no. 1 (2015): 77.

I. Abolition

1. "Women's House of Detention Protects the First Offenders," *New York Times,* March 8, 1931.

2. Audre Lorde, *Zami: A New Spelling of My Name* (Berkeley, CA: Crossing Press, 1982), 206.

3. Southerners On New Ground, "Black Mamas Bail Out Action," https:// southernersonnewground.org/our-work/freefromfear/black-mamas-bail-out-action.

4. The Bronx Freedom Fund, established in 2007 and likely the first contemporary bond fund accessible to everyday people, was discontinued in 2020, largely because some bond reforms had been implemented. See http:// www.thebronxfreedomfund.org/.

5. Joan Nestle, "Women's House of Detention, 1931–1974," Outhistory, 2008, https://outhistory.org/exhibits/show/historical-musings /womens-house-of-detention.

6. See the 1991 special edition of *Social Justice* (volume 18, no. 3), edited by Robert P. Weiss ("Attica: 1971–1991—A Commemorative Issue"). See also Heather Thompson, *Blood in the Water: The Attica Prison Uprising of 1971 and Its Legacy* (New York: Pantheon, 2016).

7. For more on this uprising see, *When the Prisoners Ran Walpole: A True Story in the Movement for Prison Abolition* by Jamie Bissonnette, Ralph Hamm, Robert Dellelo (Boston: South End Press, 2008).

8. American Friends Service Committee Working Party, *Struggle for Justice: A Report on Crime and Punishment in America* (New York: Hill and Wang, 1971), 173.

9. Prison Research Education Action Project, *Instead of Prisons: A Handbook for Abolitionists* (Syracuse: Prison Research Education Action Project,

1976), 19.

10. Fay Honey Knopp, "Radical Feminism and Abolition," *Peace Review* 6, no. 2 (1994): 203–208.

11. See the archives of the Santa Cruz Women's Prison Project at Freedom Archives, https://www.ncjrs.gov/pdffiles1/Digitization/107516NCJRS.pdf.

12. As the conversation continued, it was joined by radical philanthropist Gita Drury, who introduced the emergent organizing committee to Edwin Cohen and his Blessing Way Foundation, which provided the seed funds for the conference. For more context on Critical Resistance and this initial convening, see the 2000 special edition of *Social Justice* (volume 27, no. 3), edited by the Critical Resistance Publications Collective ("Critical Resistance to the Prison-Industrial Complex").

13. See *Captive Genders: Trans Embodiment and the Prison Industrial Complex* edited by Eric Stanley and Nat Smith (2011).

14. This thesis is elaborated in Kaaryn S. Gustafson's *Cheating Welfare: Public Assistance and the Criminalization of Poverty* (New York: New York University Press, 2011).

15. Dorothy Roberts, *Killing the Black Body: Race, Reproduction, and the Meaning of Liberty* (New York: Vintage, 1997). See also Roberts's most recent work, *Torn Apart: How the Child Welfare System Destroys Black Families—And How Abolition Can Build a Safer World* (New York: Basic Books, 2022).

16. "'Abolition Is the Only Answer': A Conversation with Dorothy Roberts," *Rise*, October 20, 2020, https://www.risemagazine.org/2020/10/conversation-with-dorothy-roberts.

17. Mike Davis, "Hell Factories in the Field: A Prison-Industrial Complex," *Nation*, February 20, 1995. See also Angela Y. Davis, "Masked Racism: Reflections on the Prison Industrial Complex," Colorlines, September 10, 1998.

18. Critical Resistance, "What Is the PIC? What Is Abolition?" http://criticalresistance.org/about/not-so-common-language/.

19. In 1974 the North Carolina Prisoners Labor Union, one of many vibrant attempts to form a labor union in prison in the 1970s, demanded an end to "the judicial-prison-parole-industrial complex." See Dan Berger and Emily

K. Hobson, *Remaking Radicalism: A Grassroots Documentary Reader of the United States, 1973–2001* (Athens: University of Georgia Press, 2020).

20.   See Angela Davis and Gina Dent, "Prison as a Border: A Conversation on Gender, Globalization, and Punishment," *Signs* 26, no. 4 "Globalization and Gender" (Summer 2001): 1235–41.

21.   Stuart Hall, et al., *Policing the Crisis: Mugging, the State, and Law and Order* (London: Macmillan, 1978).

22.   Eddie Ellis, "An Open Letter to Our Friends on the Question of Language," Center for NuLeadership on Urban Solutions, 2007, http://cmjcenter.org/wp-content/uploads/2017/07/CNUS-AppropriateLanguage.pdf.

23.   See Julia Sudbury's (now Chinyere Oparah) 2005 anthology, *Global Lockdown: Race, Gender, and the Prison-Industrial Complex* (London: Routledge), which placed campaigns and research on imprisoned women within a context that reflected the global reach of the prison industrial complex and the multiple ways in which it exploited and built upon regimes of racism and heteropatriarchy.

24.   See the Sisters Inside website at https://sistersinside.com.au.

25.   "What We Do," Canadian Association of Elizabeth Fry Societies, https://www.caefs.ca/what-we-do.

26.   See this Amnesty International Report on the campaign against F-type prisons organized by Kurdish revolutionaries: https://www.refworld.org/pdfid/3b83b70ae.pdf.

27.   Critical Resistance, "What Is the PIC? What Is Abolition?"

28.   André Gorz, *Strategy for Labor: A Radical Proposal* (Boston: Beacon Press, 1967) and Thomas Mathiesen, *The Politics of Abolition* (London: Martin Robertson and Company, 1974).

29.   Ruth Wilson Gilmore, "Making and Unmaking Mass Incarceration Conference," University of Mississippi, December 2019.

30.   Orlando Patterson, in a 1982 book, *Slavery and Social Death: A Comparative Study* (Cambridge, MA: Harvard University), offered an analysis of slavery across differing contexts, arguing that slavery aimed to produce "social death." Other scholars have built on Patterson's work to argue that criminalized communities, specifically African American ones, experience

forms of civil death. For example, after serving their sentences, people with criminal records face a network of sanctioned forms of discrimination that restrict their right to privacy, to parent, to access social benefits and other entitlements, to vote, and more. See, for example, Joan Dayan, "Legal Slaves and Civil Bodies," *Nepantla* 2, no. W, 2001, 3–39. Also see her 2011 book published as Colin Dayan, *The Law Is a White Dog: How Legal Rituals Make and Unmake Persons* (Princeton, NJ: Princeton University Press, 2011).

31. Leslie F. Goldstein, "Early Feminist Themes in French Utopian Socialism: The Saint-Simonians and Fourier," *Journal of the History of Ideas* 43, no. 1 (1982): 91–108. Republished in January 2004 in *Socialism: Critical Concepts in Political Science*, edited by Jeremy Jennings (Routledge).

32. W.E.B. Du Bois's *Black Reconstruction in America: An Essay Toward a History of the Part Which Black Folk Played in the Attempt to Reconstruct Democracy in America, 1860–1880* (New York: Free Press, 1998 [1935]).

33. Du Bois, *Black Reconstruction*, 634.

34. Du Bois, *Black Reconstruction*, 635.

35. Cheryl I. Harris, "Whiteness as Property," *Harvard Law Review*, June 10, 1993, http://harvardlawreview.org/1993/06/whiteness-as-property.

36. Paul Wright, "Slaves of the State," in *The Celling of America: An Inside Look at the U.S. Prison Industry* (Monroe, ME: Common Courage, 1998), 102. This notion derives from the prevailing opinion in Ruffin v. Commonwealth of Virginia, 62 Va 790 (1871).

37. Michelle Alexander, *The New Jim Crow: Mass Incarceration in the Age of Colorblindness* (New York: New Press, 2010); *13th*, directed by Ava DuVernay (2016, Oakland, CA: Forward Movement).

38. See Anna Mae Duane and Erica Meiners, "Working Analogies: Slavery Now and Then," in *Fighting Modern Slavery and Human Trafficking: History and Contemporary Policy*, edited by Jessica Pliley, Genevieve LeBaron, and David W. Blight (Cambridge, UK: Cambridge University Press, 2021).

39. Robert Perkinson, *Texas Tough: The Rise of America's Prison Empire* (New York: Henry Holt, 2010).

40. See the Polaris Project (https://polarisproject.org/) and Julie Bindel, *The Pimping of Prostitution: Abolishing the Sex Work Myth* (London: Palgrave, 2017).

41. See Aja Romano, "A New Law Intended to Curb Sex Trafficking Threatens the Future of the Internet as We Know It," Vox, July 2, 2018, https://www.vox.com/culture/2018/4/13/17172762/fosta-sesta-backpage-230-internet-freedom; and Liz Tung, "FOSTA-SESTA Was Supposed to Thwart Sex Trafficking. Instead, It's Sparked a Movement," PBS, July 10, 2020, https://whyy.org/segments/fosta-sesta-was-supposed-to-thwart-sex-trafficking-instead-its-sparked-a-movement/.

42. See, for example, Dylan Rodríguez, "'Mass Incarceration' as Misnomer," *The Abolitionist,* https://abolitionistpaper.files.wordpress.com/2017/04/the-abolitionist-issue-26.pdf

43. See German Lopez, "The First Step Act, Explained," Vox, February 5, 2019, https://www.vox.com/future-perfect/2018/12/18/18140973/state-of-the-union-trump-first-step act-criminal-justice-reform.

44. This phrase resounds from the work of Saidiya Hartman. See *Wayward Lives, Beautiful Experiments: Intimate Histories of Riotous Black Girls, Troublesome Women, and Queer Radicals* (New York: Norton, 2019).

45. Kerwin Kaye, *Enforcing Freedom: Drug Courts, Therapeutic Communities, and the Intimacies of the State* (New York: Columbia University Press, 2019).

46. Liat Ben-Moshe, *Decarcerating Disability: Deinstitutionalization and Prison Abolition* (Minneapolis: University of Minnesota Press, 2020).

47. Annie Lowrey, "Her Only Crime Was Helping Her Kids," *Atlantic,* September 13, 2019, https://www.theatlantic.com/ideas/archive/2019/09/her-only-crime-was-helping-her-kid/597979/.

48. Francisco Aviles Pino "LA County Votes to Stop Construction of New Jail-Like Facility," *The Intercept,* August 22, 2019, https://theintercept.com/2019/08/22/los-angeles-county-mental-health-facility-abolition/

49. James Kilgore, "Repackaging Mass Incarceration," Counterpunch, June 6, 2014, https://www.counterpunch.org/2014/06/06/repackaging-mass-incarceration.

50. Antonio Pacheco, "Interrogating the Impacts of NYC's Rikers Jail Replacement Plan," Archinect News, December 12, 2019, https://archinect.com/news/article/150174335/interrogating-the-impacts-of-nyc-s-rikers-jail-replacement-plan.

51. Jackie Wang, *Carceral Capitalism* (Cambridge, MA: MIT Press, 2018).

52. For more on this campaign, see Osha Oneeka Daya Brown, Lee Doane, Sterling Fleming, Hakim Trent, Jeremy Valerio, and Outside Organizers with No New Jails NYC, "$11 Billion for What?! Incarcerated Organizers with No New Jails NYC Explain How to Shut Down Rikers Without Building New Jails," *CUNY Law Review*, March 20, 2020.

53. In 1969, in *Black Awakening in Capitalist America* (New York: Doubleday, 1969), Robert Allen named the role white philanthropy played in managing political insurgencies, particularly Black Power movements. In the 1980s the Ford Foundation, Field Foundation, and other large foundations moved aggressively to redirect farmworker organizing away from "militant" actions such as strikes and direct action to projects centered on educational support and service provision. In 2019, as the power of largely female and often non-white teachers' unions surged, the Eli and Edythe Broad and Bill and Melinda Gates Foundations pumped resources into their top-down and anti-labor versions of K–12 educational reform.

II. Feminism

1. "Moment of Truth: Statement of Commitment to Black Lives," June 30, 2020, https://wscadv.org/news/moment-of-truth.

2. Tommy Simmons, "Law Enforcement Groups Withdraw Support of Idaho Coalition Over Letter Calling for Racial Justice," *Idaho State Journal*, October 21, 2020, https://www.idahostatejournal.com/news/local/law-en-forcement-groups-withdraw-support-of-idaho-coalition-over-letter-calling-for-racial-justice/article_cef47a44-5de3-55f7-9998-3f17ef458777.html.

3. Embrace, "Embrace Supports Communities of Color," https://www.documentcloud.org/documents/20398151-embrace-statement-on-supporting-communities-of-color.

4. Melissa Gira Grant, "An Anti-Rape Movement Without Police," *New Republic*, October 20, 2020, https://newrepublic.com/article/159850/anti-rape-movement-without-police.

5. Casey Gwinn and Gael Strack, "Another Perspective on 'The Moment of Truth,'" *Domestic Violence Report* 26, no. 2 (December/January 2021): 17–21.

6.   See, for example, Donna Coker, "Why Opposing Hyper-incarceration Should Be Central to the Work of Anti-Domestic Violence Movement," *University of Miami Race and Social Justice Law Review* 585 (2015), and Mimi Kim, "Challenging the Pursuit of Criminalization in an Era of Mass Incarceration: The Limits of Social Work Response to Domestic Violence in the US," *British Journal of Social Work*, 2015.

7.   The founding members of INCITE! were Sandra Comacho, Jamie Lee Evans, Michelle Erai, Kata Issari, Jamie Jimenez, Isabel Kang, Valli Kalei Kanuha, Mimi Kim, Kelley Mitchell-Clark, Beth E. Richie, Loretta Rivera, Ana Clarissa Rojas Durazo, Andrea Smith, Nan Stoops, Sharon Todd, Janelle White, and Sherry Wilson.

8.   Beth E. Richie, *Arrested Justice: Black Women, Violence, and America's Prison Nation* (New York: New York University Press, 2016); Susan Schechter, *Women and Male Violence: The Visions and Struggles of the Battered Women's Movement* (Boston: South End Press, 1982).

9.   Lisa Levenstein, *They Didn't See Us Coming: The Hidden History of Feminism in the Nineties* (New York: New York: Basic Books, 2020); Ann Russo, *Feminist Accountability: Disrupting Violence and Transforming Power* (New York University Press, 2018); Beth Richie, Val Kalei Kanuha, and Kayla Martensen, "Colluding With and Resisting the State: Organizing Against Gender Violence in the U.S.," *Feminist Criminology*, January 19, 2021, https://doi:10.1177/1557085120987607.

10.   Robin McDuff, Deanne Pernell, and Karen Saunders, "Letter to the Anti-Rape Movement," *Off Our Backs* 7, no. 5 (June 1977): 9–10.

11.   If conventional genealogies of anti-violence activism are being productively contested, so too are studies of the historical linkages of racism and punishment. Sarah Haley's *No Mercy Here: Gender, Punishment and Jim Crow Modernity* (Chapel Hill: University of North Carolina Press, 2016) chronicles how late nineteenth-century and early twentieth-century practices of incarceration shaped gendered and racialized logics. It serves as a compelling example of what it means to develop rich interdisciplinary research and analyses that are grounded in antiracist and feminist theories and practices. Her book might be characterized as abolition feminism at work.

12. Fran Beal, "Double Jeopardy: To Be Black and Female," in Toni Cade, ed., *The Black Woman: An Anthology* (New York: New American Library Publishers, 1970) and in Robin Morgan, *Sisterhood Is Powerful* (New York: Vintage, 1970); Claudia Jones, "An End to the Neglect of the Problems of the Negro Woman!" *Political Affairs* 28, no. 6 (1949): 51–67.

13. Esther Cooper Jackson, "The Negro Domestic Worker in Relation to Trade Unionism," (Masters thesis, Fisk University, 1940). Republished in Viewpoint Magazine, October 31, 2015, https://viewpointmag.com/2015/10/31/the-negro-woman-domestic-worker-in-relation-to-trade-unionism-1940.

14. Ella Baker and Marvel Cooke, "Bronx Slave Market," *The Crisis*, November 1935: 330–32.

15. Brandi Jackson, "No Ground on Which to Stand: Revise Your Stand Your Ground Laws So Survivors of Domestic Violence Are No Longer Incarcerated for Defending their Lives," *Berkeley Journal of Gender, Law and Justice* 154 (2015); Barbara L. Zust, "Assessing and Addressing Domestic Violence Experienced by Incarcerated Women," *Creative Nursing: Social Justice and Nursing* 14, no. 2.

16. Committee on Domestic Violence and Incarcerated Women, "Battered Women and Criminal Justice: A Report of the Committee on Domestic Violence and Incarcerated Women," June 1987, https://www.ojp.gov/pdffiles1/Digitization/107516NCJRS.pdf.

17. See the Santa Cruz Women's Prison Project Newsletter, February 1974, at http://freedomarchives.org/Documents/Finder/DOC70_scans/70SCWPP.Newsletter.Feb1974.pdf..

18. These organizations were (and are) supported by abolition feminists like Alisa Bierria, Kathy Boudin, Rachel Caidor, Monica Cosby, Andrea James, Mariame Kaba, Mimi Kim, Colby Lenz, Miss Major, Colette Payne, Cassandra Shaylor, Gail Smith, and Dean Spade.

19. Beth E. Richie, *Compelled to Crime: The Gender Entrapment of Battered Black Women* (New York: Routledge, 1996); Karlene Faith, *Unruly Women: The Politics of Confinement & Resistance* (New York: Seven Stories Press, 2011 [1993]); Paula Johnson, *Inner Lives: Voices of African American Women in Prison* (New York: NYU Press, 2004).

20. Beth Richie and Kayla Martensen, "Resisting Carcerality, Embracing Abolition: Implications for Social Work Practice," *Affilia* 35, no. 11 (2020).

21. See, for example, discussion of the NPIC in the INCITE!-authored anthology *The Revolution Will Not Be Funded: Beyond the Non-Profit Industrial Complex* (Durham, NC: Duke University Press, 2017).

22. Mimi E. Kim, "The Carceral Creep: Gender-Based Violence, Race and the Expansion of the Punitive State, 1973–1983," *Social Problems* 67, no. 2 (2020): 251–69.

23. Alisa Bierria, "Pursuing A Radical Anti-Violence Agenda Inside/Outside a Non-Profit Structure." In Incite! Women of Color Against Violence (Ed.), *The Revolution Will Not Be Funded,* 151–163.

24. "National Intimate Partner and Sexual Violence Survey Summary Report," National Center for Injury Prevention and Control of the Center for Diseases Control, 2010.

25. Violent Crime Control and Law Enforcement Act of 1994, US Department of Justice Fact Sheet, https://www.ncjrs.gov/txtfiles/billfs.txt.

26. Mari Matsuda, "Crime and Punishment," *Ms. Magazine,* November/December 1994, 86–88.

27. Mimi E. Kim, "VAWA @ 20: The Mainstreaming of the Criminalization Critique: Reflections on VAWA 20 Years Later," *City University of New York Law Review* 18, no. 1 (2014): 52–57.

28. Kim, "Carceral Creep," 251.

29. The term "carceral feminism" was originally developed by Elizabeth Bernstein in the context of her analysis of anti-trafficking efforts. "The Sexual Politics of the 'New Abolitionism,'" *differences* 18, no. 3 (2007): 128–51.

30. Anannya Bhattacharjee, "Whose Safety? Women of Color and the Violence of Law Enforcement," American Friends Service Committee, Committee on Women, Population, and the Environment, 2001, https://www.afsc.org/sites/default/files/documents/whose%20safety.pdf.

31. See, for example, Anne Braden, "Free Thomas Wansley: A Letter to White Southern Women" (Louisville: SCEF Press, 1972), at https://newsreel.org/guides/Anne-Braden-A-Letter-to-White-Southern-Women.pdf; and Ida B. Wells Barnett, *The Red Record: Tabulated Statistics and Alleged Causes of Lynching in the United States, 1892–1894* (reprint, CreateSpace

Independent Publishing Platform, 2015).

32. There is considerable debate about this question. For a good summary of the argument, particularly as it is linked to questions of structural racism and policing, see Survived & Punished #Set Them Free website: https://survivedandpunished.org. Another good summary source is Meg Aprill's *Why Domestic Violence Survivors Fear Turning to the Police*, at http://www.dayoneny.org/blog/2020/8/5/why-domestic-violence-survivors-fearnbsp-turning-to-the-police.

33. Angela Y. Davis, *Freedom Is a Constant Struggle: Ferguson, Palestine, and the Foundations of a Movement* (Chicago: Haymarket Books, 2015).

34. The 2021 version, which was being considered as this book was going to press, included a provision for restorative justice, which many mainstream organizations supported, thereby fortifying carceral expansion and commitment to the criminal legal system.

35. Connor Friedersdorf, "Police Have a Much Bigger Domestic-Abuse Problem Than the NFL Does," *Atlantic*, September 19, 2014, https://www.theatlantic.com/national/archive/2014/09/police-officers-who-hit-their-wives-or-girlfriends/380329. And Leigh Goodmark, "Hands up at Home: Militarized Masculinity and Police Officers Who Commit Intimate Partner Abuse," *BYU Law Review 2015 (5)*.

36. As cited in Melissa Jeltsen, "Don't Use Domestic Violence Victims to Derail Police Reform," July 20, 2020, domesticshelters.org, https://www.domesticshelters.org/articles/in-the-news/don-t-use-domestic-violence-victims-to-derail-police-reform.

37. Congressional Research Service, "The Violence Against Women Act (VAWA): Historical Overview, Funding, and Reauthorization," April 23, 2019, https://fas.org/sgp/crs/misc/R45410.pdf.

38. See the She Safe, We Safe campaign at https://www.shesafewesafe.org.

39. Dorothy Roberts, *Torn Apart: How the Child Welfare System Destroys Black Families—and How Abolition Can Build a Safer World*, forthcoming from New York: Basic Books, 2022, page 40.

40. See Flat Out, http://www.flatout.org.au.

41. Calla Wahlquist, "Crowdfunding Campaign to Free Indigenous Women 'Shocked' by WA Response," *Guardian*, January 22, 2019, https://www.

theguardian.com/australia-news/2019/jan/23/crowdfunding-cam-paign-to-free-indigenous-women-shocked-by-wa-government-response.

42.   Sohela Surajpal, "Carceral Feminism Is Not the Answer," Africa Is a Country, https://africasacountry.com/2020/09/carceral-feminism-is-not-the-answer.

43.   "Sisters Uncut Stands in Solidary with the Wet'suwet'en," February 20, 2020, https://www.sistersuncut.org/2020/02/20/sisters-un-cut-stands-in-solidarity-with-the-wetsuweten.

44.   Maureen Mansfield, "What Is Abolition Feminism, and Why Does It Matter?" IPPR Progressive Review, June 13, 2018, https://www.ippr.org/juncture-item/what-is-abolitionist-feminism-and-why-does-it-matter.

III. Now

1.   While the number of people in some jails declined during the coronavirus pandemic, according to the Prison Policy Institute (PPI), in the summer of 2020, prisons were "releasing almost no one." PPI tracked COVID-19 relat-ed prison releases (and fatalities) in the United States. See "The Most Sig-nificant Criminal Justice Policy Changes from the COVID-19 Pandemic," May 18, 2021, https://www.prisonpolicy.org/virus/virusresponse.html. See also DLA Piper and Association for the Prevention of Torture, "A Glob-al Analysis of Prisoner Releases in Response to COVID-19," December 2020, www.dlapiper.com/~/media/files/insights/publications/2021/03/dla-piper-prison-population-during-covid-19.pdf?la=en&hash=F5C1EB-BA0D3D86BDDA58FAC87DB9EF3CAE3815DF.

2.   Ruth Wilson Gilmore has defined racism as "the state-sanctioned and/or extralegal production and exploitation of group-differentiated vulnera-bility to premature death." See Golden Gulag: Prisons, Surplus, Crisis, and Opposition in Globalizing California (Berkeley: University of California Press, 2007), 247. In addition to the matter of premature death, aging is also accelerated for people living in prisons, even as age is a contested con-cept. Across the United States prisons do not possess a uniform age marker for an "old," "elderly," or "aging" person, which impacts data collection and also constrains organizing. While limited, an emerging body of research

illustrates that at approximately age fifty, people in prison begin to display
health related challenges usually associated with someone much older.
See, for example, Maurice Chammah, "Do You Age Faster in Prison?,"
Marshall Project, August 24, 2015, https://www.themarshallproject.
org/2015/08/24/do-you-age-faster-in-prison.

3. "Inside Prison amid Coronavirus Pandemic: Incarcerated Journal-
    ist Says Millions Behind Bars at Risk," interview with Juan Moreno
    Haines, *Democracy Now!*, March 17, 2020, https://www.democracynow.
    org/2020/3/17/coronavirus_prisons_san_quentin.

4. Gloria Anzaldúa, *Borderlands/La Frontera: The New Mestiza* (San Francis-
    co: Aunt Lute, 1987), 109.

5. See, for example, adrienne maree brown's *Emergent Strategies: Shaping
    Change, Changing Worlds* (Chico, CA: AK Press, 2017) for a robust discus-
    sion of scale and social movements.

6. Bryan Stevenson and Gina Dent, "Images, Memory, and Justice," Visualiz-
    ing Abolition, Institute of the Arts and Sciences, University of California,
    Santa Cruz, October 27, 2020, https://visualizingabolition.ucsc.edu.
    exhibitions/visualizing-abolition.html.

7. Stephanie Woodard, "The Police Killings No One Is Talking About," *In
    These Times*, October 17, 2016, https://inthesetimes.com/features/native_
    american_police_killings_native_lives_matter.html.

8. National Center for Transgender Equality, "The Report of the US Trans-
    gender Survey Executive Summary," December 2016, https://transequality.
    org/sites/default/files/docs/usts/USTS-Executive-Summary-Dec17.pdf.

9. See Flint Taylor, "How Activists Won Reparations for the Survivors of
    Chicago Police Department Torture," *In These Times*, June 26, 2015,
    http://inthesetimes.com/article/18118/jon-burge-torture-reparations;
    Alice Kim, "Breaking Walls: Lessons from Chicago," in *The Long Term:
    Resisting Life Sentences, Working Toward Freedom*, edited by Alice Kim,
    Erica R. Meiners, Audrey Petty, Jilly Petty, Beth E. Richie, and Sarah Ross
    (Chicago: Haymarket Books, 2018).

10. "We Charge Genocide, Police Violence against Chicago's Youth of Color:
    A Report Prepared for the United Nations Committee against Torture,"
    September 2014, http://report.wechargegenocide.org.

11. For more on Chicago's policing budget see, for example, "What is the Chicago Police Department Budget?," June 23, 2020, https://www.civ-icfed.org/civic-federation/blog/what-chicago-police-department-bud-get. This is not unique to Chicago. See, for example, the analysis of the percentage of Canadian municipal budgets spent on policing and per capita spending in Tom Cordoso and Molly Hayes, "Canadian Cities' Po-lice Spending Ranges from One 10th to Nearly a Third of Total Budgets, Globe Analysis Finds," *Globe and Mail*, August 16, 2020, https://www. theglobeandmail.com/canada/article-canadian-cities-police-spend-ing-ranges-from-one-10th-to-nearly-a/?fbclid=IwAR01RaMqqKluvsX-mD1XJjBHnAbOHTxKDa6AsUhVB4isjKiuP6NAXJzPD0hI.

12. Hill was also known by "Breonna "Be'Be" Hill.

13. Andrea Ritchie, *Invisible No More: Police Violence Against Black Women and Women of Color* (Boston: Beacon Press, 2017).

14. Elizabeth Alexander, "The Trayvon Generation," *New Yorker*, June 15, 2020.

15. In the 1960s, in an effort to monitor policing, the Chicago Police De-partment implemented an experimental initiative where some police audiotaped their interactions with people. Gay liberation organizations, pushing back on routine police harassment and entrapment and this "Stop and Quiz" mandate, ruefully described this reform option in a 1960s Chicago gay newsletter, *Mattachine Midwest*: "So, if you're lucky enough to be stopped while on tape, remember to speak clearly." See Therese Quinn and Erica R. Meiners, "Good Cop? Bad Cop? No Cop! Queer Resistance to Policing," *Windy City Times*, July 29, 2015.

16. YWEP was started by Claudine O'Leary. Key YWEP organizers and com-munity members included Shira Hassan, Tanuja Jagernauth, Laura Mintz, Dominique McKinney, C. Angel Torres, Naima Paz, and Cindy Ibarra.

17. These groups were supported by adult allies like Kay Barrett, Lara Brooks, Rachel Caidor, Jen Curly, Stacy Erenberg, Mia Henry, Mariame Kaba, Manju Rajendra, Ann Russo, Mary Scott-Boria, Melissa Spatz, Salamishah Tillet, and Scheherazade Tillet.

18. Ann Russo and Melissa Spatz, "Communities Engaged in Resisting Vio-lence," Women & Girls Collective Action Network, 2008, https://comm-org.wisc.edu/papers2008/russo.htm#What_You_Can_Do!.

19. Jenny Simeone-Casas and Sarah Conway, "Grandmothers of Chicago's Restorative Justice Movement," City Bureau, January 3, 2018, https://www.citybureau.org/stories/2018/3/1/grandmothers-of-chicagos-restorative-justice-movement.

20. Savannah Shange has pointed to similar dynamics for San Francisco—*Progressive Dystopia: Abolition, Antiblackness, and Schooling in San Francisco* (Durham, NC: Duke University Press, 2019).

21. Karen Lynn Morton and Felipa Mena coordinated and advanced a lot of *Community Organizing and Family Issues*' restorative justice work with families and parents. See the "Parent-to-Parent Guide: Restorative Justice in Chicago Public Schools," Community Organizing and Family Issues, December 2015, http://www.cofionline.org/COFI/wp-content/uploads/2016/06/COFI-P2P-guide-update-2015.pdf.

22. Dorothy Roberts, "Abolishing Policing Also Means Abolishing Family Regulation," Imprint, June 16, 2020, https://imprintnews.org/child-welfare-2/abolishing-policing-also-means-abolishing-family-regulation/44480?fbclid=IwAR1vfOAeWs9vZ1ZhAfCCyC5WPoSjPMXbQ6g8vJkV9x7rPklfBQ-AgD1WIX4. See also https://www.risemagazine.org/2020/10/conversation-with-dorothy-roberts.

23. Immigrant Youth Justice League was started by Chicago area undocumented youth, including Rigo Padilla, Tania Unzueta, and Rey Wences.

24. Initially proposed in 2001, the Development, Relief, and Education for Alien Minors Act (DREAM Act) essentially would provide some eligible undocumented young people who arrived in the US under the age of sixteen years old with no criminal records and "good moral character" limited and temporary relief from deportation and potentially, for some, a pathway towards US citizenship. Versions of this Act have been repeatedly introduced over the last two decades but have never passed.

25. In April 2021, at a gathering organized by the Institute for Research on Race and Public Policy, "Forced Out," Chicago area organizations and networks working against deportation and incarceration shared analysis and strategies.

26. Key organizers of Visible Voices included Colette Payne and Joanne Archibald.

27. Andrea J. Ritchie and Joey L. Mogul, "In the Shadows of the War on Terror: Persistent Police Brutality and Abuse of People of Color in the United States: A Report Prepared for the United Nations Committee on the Elimination of Racial Discrimination," *DePaul Journal for Social Justice* 1, no. 2 (2008): 175–250.

28. See the Love & Protect website for more on their mission and practice: https://loveprotect.org/misson.

29. Survivors for Divestment, http://www.defendsurvivorsnow.org/survivors-for-divestment.

30. N.W.A's 1988 song "Fuck tha Police" on the album *Straight Outta Compton* was an indictment of the violence of policing, and it reemerged in 2014 as an anthem to accompany the murder of Michael Brown in Ferguson.

31. Laura Moser, "The Awkward Radicalization of the Chicago Teacher's Union," Slate, April 7, 2016, https://slate.com/human-interest/2016/04/chicago-teachers-union-is-going-through-an-awkward-radicalization.html.

32. Kristian Williams, *Our Enemies in Blue: Police and Power in America* (Oakland, CA: AK Press, 2015).

33. Wes Venteicher, "'No Evident Justification' for California Prison Guard Raises in Contract, Analyst Warns," *Sacramento Bee*, June 17, 2019, https://www.sacbee.com/news/politics-government/the-state-worker/article231649048.htm.

34. Kenneth Quinnell, "Get to Know AFL-CIO's Affiliates: International Union of Police Associations," AFL-CIO, September 23, 2019, https://aflcio.org/2019/9/23/get-know-afl-cios-affiliates-international-union-police-associations.

35. When the campaign to close Rikers in New York City seemed on the verge of success, it was announced that four new jails would be constructed to take the place of the jails on Rikers Island. Ford Foundation Fellows and others who criticized Darren Walker, president of the Ford Foundation, for his support of this plan and participation in the decision-making process were admonished for their "acrimony."

36. Audre Lorde, "The Uses of Anger: Women Responding to Racism," in *Sister Outsider: Essays and Speeches* (Berkeley, CA: Crossing Press, 1984), 124–33.

37. Lorde, "Uses of Anger," 127.

38. Sarah Karp, "Black Teachers Hit Harder by CPS Layoffs," Better Government Association, September 2, 2015, https://www.bettergov.org/news/black-teachers-hit-harder-by-cps-layoffs.

39. See, for example, Charles R. Hale, ed., *Engaging Contradictions: Theory, Politics, and Methos of Activist Scholarship* (Berkeley: University of California Press: 2008), https://shifter-magazine.com/wp-content/uploads/2015/10/Gilmore-Forgotten-Places.pdf; David Harvey, *The Limits to Capital* (London: Verso, 2018).

40. Benji Hart, "Misogyny on the Mag Mile: A Turning Point," Radical Faggot, December 2, 2015, https://radfag.com/2015/12/02/misogyny-on-the-mag-mile-a-turning-point.

41. See "The Chicago Gang Database," Erase the Database, September 2018, http://erasethedatabase.com/wp-content/uploads/2018/09/Chicago-Gang-Database-Proposed-Ordinance.pdf.

42. See, for example, Alex Vitale, *The End of Policing* (Brooklyn: Verso, 2017) and Beth Richie, Dylan Rodríguez, Mariame Kaba, Melissa Burch, Rachel Herzing, and Shana Agid, "Problems with Community Control of Police and Proposals for Alternatives," https://static1.squarespace.com/static/5ee39ec764dbd7179cf1243c/t/6008c586b43eee58a4c-4b73e/1611187590375/Problems+with+Community+Control.pdf.

43. See Erica Meiners, "Never Innocent: Feminist Trouble with Sex Offender Registries and Protection in a Prison Nation," in *Meridians Volume 9*, No. 2 (2008).

44. Rose Braz, "Kinder, Gentler, Gender Responsive Cages: Prison Expansion Is Not Prison Reform," *Women, Girls & Criminal Justice* (October/November 2006): 87–91.

45. Jordan T. Camp and Christina Heatherton, "How Liberals Legitimate Broken Windows: An Interview with Naomi Murakawa," in *Policing the Planet: Why the Policing Crisis Led to Black Lives Matter*, edited by Jordan T. Camp and Christina Heatherton (New York: Verso Books, 2016), 227–36.

46. Paul Biasco and Mitchell Armentrout, "Police Union Blasts 'Sham Trial and Shameful' Van Dyke Guilty Verdict," *Chicago Sun Times*, October 5, 2018, https://chicago.suntimes.com/2018/10/5/18460941/police-union-

blasts-sham-trial-and-shameful-van-dyke-guilty-verdict.

47. John Byrne, "Mayor Rahm Emanuel Announces Next Step in Police Acad-
      emy Project, a Plan That Continues to Draw Criticism," *Chicago Tribune*,
      November 16, 2018, https://www.chicagotribune.com/politics/ct-met-
      rahm-emanuel-police-academy-20181116-story.html.

48. Benji Hart, "How #NoCopAcademy Shook the Machine," *Chicago Reader*,
      April 26, 2019, https://www.chicagoreader.com/chicago/how-nocopacad-
      emy-shook-the-machine/Content?oid=69862164.

49. Micol Siegel, *Violence Work: State Power and the Limits of Police* (Durham,
      NC: Duke University Press, 2018), 7.

50. Bernice Johnson Reagon, "Coalition Politics: Turning the Century," in
      Home Girls: A Black Feminist Anthology, edited by Barbara Smith (New
      York: Kitchen Table Press, 1983), 343–56.

51. Saidiya Hartman, *Wayward Lives, Beautiful Experiments: Intimate Histories
      of Riotous Black Girls, Troublesome Women, and Queer Radicals* (New York:
      Norton, 2019), 33.

52. See the work of the Rasmea Defense Committee at http://justice4rasmea.
      org/.

53. For more on learned ignorance, see Eve Kosofsky Sedgwick, *Epistemol-
      ogy of the Closet* (Cambridge, MA: Harvard University Press, 1990), and
      Charles Mills, *The Racial Contract* (Ithaca, NY: Cornell University Press,
      1997).

54. In 2020 Illinois governor Pritzker announced the planned closure of
      five large state prisons for young people and the "transformation" of the
      juvenile justice system in Illinois. See Heather Cherone, "Pritzker Unveils
      Plan to 'Transform' Juvenile Justice in Illinois by Closing Large Facilities,"
      WTTW News, July 31, 2020, https://news.wttw.com/2020/07/31/pritz-
      ker-unveils-plan-transform-juvenile-justice-illinois-closing-large-facilities.

55. Mimi E. Kim, "Anti-Carceral Feminism: The Contradictions of Progress
      and the Possibilities of Counter-Hegemonic Struggle," *Affilia* 35, no. 3
      (2020): 309–26.

56. See the Twitter page of the Chicago Police Department's Office of Restor-
      ative Justice Strategies at https://twitter.com/cpd_rj?lang=en.

57. For more on Illinois prison population, review data reports from the Vera

Institute of Justice, https://www.vera.org/downloads/pdfdownloads/state-incarceration-trends-illinois.pdf ; and Prison Policy Institute https://www.prisonpolicy.org/profiles/IL.html.

58. Lorraine Swanson, "Tiffany Van Dyke: 'I Can't Bury My Husband,'" Patch.com, February 14, 2019, https://patch.com/illinois/chicago/wife-says-she-was-kept-dark-jason-van-dyke-s-beating.

59. Dahleen Glanton, "We Can't Blame Tiffany Van Dyke for Trying, but Her Husband Is Just Another Convicted Felon," *Chicago Tribune*, February 16, 2019, https://www.chicagotribune.com/columns/dahleen-glanton/ct-met-dahleen-glanton-jason-van-dyke-beating-20190215-story.html.

60. From 1969 to 1973, an underground network, the Jane Collective, provided women in Chicago access to safe abortions. From 1995 to 2015, Amigas Latinas supported and advocated for Latina lesbian, bisexual, transgender, and questioning women across Chicago.

61. Gwendolyn Brooks, "Paul Robeson," from *Blacks* (Chicago: Third World Press, 1984).

Epilogue

1. Mohamed Shehk, Pilar Weiss, Rachel Foran, Sharlyn Grace, and Woods Ervin, "On the Road to Freedom: An Abolitionist Assessment of Pretrial and Bail Reforms," Critical Resistance, June 2021, http://criticalresistance.org/wp-content/uploads/2021/07/OnTheRoadToFreedom_FINAL_June2021-compressed.pdf.

2. Audre Lorde, "Learning from the 60s," address for Malcolm X celebration at Harvard University, February 1982.

3. Liza Featherstone, "Elite Feminists Ran Cover for Andrew Cuomo," *Jacobin*, August 12, 2021, https://jacobinmag.com/2021/08/elite-liberal-feminism-times-up-roberta-kaplan-andrew-cuomo-metoo.

IMAGE PERMISSIONS

Illustration of science fiction's radical imaginative potential published by permission of Ira M. Leigh, iramleigh.com.

Graphic depicting demands of #8toAbolition published by permission of the campaign co-creaters.

Free CeCe McDonald poster and poster for Eisha Love by Micah Bazant. Published by permission of the artist.

Cover of *Reimagining Justice in South Africa Beyond Policing* by Mikayla Boorany. Published by permission of the artist.

Marielle Presente poster published by permission from Anielle Franco.

Graphic for Black Mamas Bail Out Action by Micky Jordan. Published by permission of the artist and Southerners on New Ground.

1998 Critical Resistance conference poster published by permission of the Rupert Garcia and Rena Bransten Gallery.

Study, poster for the Critical Resistance 2008 conference, by Pete Railand. Published by permission of the artist.

Free Our Queens published by permission of Melanie Cervantes. More info at: www.peoplespaperco-op.com and https://dignidadrebelde.com.

Building Freedom Behind Bars poster by Alexander Dwinell and Sanya Hyland, National Prisoners Reform Association, Celebrate People's History Poster Series no. 68, December 2010. Published by permission of the artists. Available at https://justseeds.org/product/national-prisoners-reform-association.

Stop the Raids poster by Jesus Barraza. Published by permission of the artist. Available at https://dignidadrebelde.com/stop-the-raids.

Reformist Reforms vs. Abolitionist Steps to End Imprisonment poster is part of the Abolitionist Steps poster series available at: http://criticalresistance.org/resources/abolitionist-tools. Published by permission of Critical Resistance.

INCITE! illustration © Cristy C. Road. Published by permission of the artist. https://www.croadcore.org.

Dandelions & Butterflies by art twink published by permission of the artist.

Third World Women's Alliance newsletter, *Triple Jeopardy* 1, no. 1, September–October 1971, published by permission of Smith College Special Collections, Third World Women's Alliance, Bay Area chapter records, Box 7, Folder 2.

"Open Letter to the Anti-Rape Movement" written by Robin McDuff, Deanne Pernell, and Karen Saunders, published in *Off Our Backs* 7, no. 5, June 1997.

"Prison Is Not Feminist" button published by permission of Project Nia.

Intimate Partner Violence and State Violence Power and Control Wheel published by permission of Monica Cosby and Sarah Ross.

Poster by Centre for the Human Rights of Imprisoned People (CHRIP) Working Group, a project of Flat Out, published by permission of Flat Out. Poster design by Emma Russell, Phoebe Barton, Lorena Solin, Amanda George, Vicki Roach, Annie Nash and Helena (last name withheld on request). Illustrations by Rachel Barrett. Depicted in poster are organizers from a range of networks in Australia (left to right): Annie Nash, Helena, Vicki Roach, Amanda George, and Lorena Solin.

Free Marissa Alexander poster by Molly Crabapple published by permission of Love & Protect.

Untitled by Joseph Dole used by permission of Shari Stone-Mediatore.

Sounds of Abolition, Love & Protect logo, and poster for Chicago abolition events by Monica Trinidad, http://www.monicatrinidad.com. Published by permission of the artist.

Cover of *No Good Prosecutors—Now or Ever* pamphlet by Jett George. Published by permission of Survived & Punished.

Coins, Cops, and Communities Toolkit published by permission of AFSC Chicago.

Networkers, 2021, published by permission of Molly Costello.

INDEX

ABOUT HAYMARKET BOOKS

Haymarket Books is a radical, independent, nonprofit book publisher based in Chicago. Our mission is to publish books that contribute to struggles for social and economic justice. We strive to make our books a vibrant and organic part of social movements and the education and development of a critical, engaged, international left.

We take inspiration and courage from our namesakes, the Haymarket martyrs, who gave their lives fighting for a better world. Their 1886 struggle for the eight-hour day—which gave us May Day, the international workers' holiday—reminds workers around the world that ordinary people can organize and struggle for their own liberation. These struggles continue today across the globe—struggles against oppression, exploitation, poverty, and war.

Since our founding in 2001, Haymarket Books has published more than five hundred titles. Radically independent, we seek to drive a wedge into the risk-averse world of corporate book publishing. Our authors include Noam Chomsky, Arundhati Roy, Rebecca Solnit, Angela Y. Davis, Howard Zinn, Amy Goodman, Wallace Shawn, Mike Davis, Winona LaDuke, Ilan Pappé, Richard Wolff, Dave Zirin, Keeanga-Yamahtta Taylor, Nick Turse, Dahr Jamail, David Barsamian, Elizabeth Laird, Amira Hass, Mark Steel, Avi Lewis, Naomi Klein, and Neil Davidson. We are also the trade publishers of the acclaimed Historical Materialism Book Series and of Dispatch Books.

ALSO AVAILABLE FROM HAYMARKET BOOKS

Angela Davis: An Autobiography
Angela Y. Davis

*Border and Rule: Global Migration, Capitalism,
and the Rise of Racist Nationalism*
Harsha Walia, foreword by Robin D. G. Kelley,
afterword by Nick Estes

*The Brother You Choose: Paul Coates and Eddie Conway Talk About
Life, Politics, and The Revolution*
Susie Day. afterword by Ta-Nehisi Coates

*Freedom Is a Constant Struggle: Ferguson, Palestine, and the Foun-
dations of a Movement*
Angela Y. Davis, edited by Frank Barat, preface by Cornel West

From #BlackLivesMatter to Black Liberation
Keeanga-Yamahtta Taylor, foreword by Angela Y. Davis

The Long Term: Resisting Life Sentences Working Toward Freedom
Edited by Alice Kim, Erica R. Meiners, Jill Petty, Audrey Petty,
Beth E. Richie, and Sarah Ross

I Am Troy Davis
Troy Davis, Martina Davis-Correia, and Jen Marlowe, foreword
by Helen Prejean

A Time to Die: The Attica Prison Revolt
Tom Wicker

ABOUT THE AUTHORS

Angela Y. Davis is professor emerita of history of consciousness and feminist studies at University of California, Santa Cruz. An activist, writer, and lecturer, her work focuses on prisons, police, abolition and the related intersections of race, gender, and class. She is the author of many books, from *Angela Davis: An Autobiography* to *Freedom is a Constant Struggle*.

Gina Dent is associate professor of feminist studies, history of consciousness, and legal studies at University of California, Santa Cruz. She is the editor of *Black Popular Culture* and lectures and writes on African diaspora literary and cultural studies, postcolonial theory, and critical area studies. Her current project, Visualizing Abolition (www. visualizingabolition.ucsc.edu), grows out of her work as an advocate for transformative and transitional justice and prison abolition.

Erica R. Meiners is a professor of education and women's, gender, and sexuality studies at Northeastern Illinois University. A writer, organizer and educator, Meiners is the author *For the Children? Protecting Innocence in a Carceral State,* coauthor of *The Feminist and the Sex Offender: Confronting Sexual Harm, Ending State Violence,* and a coeditor of *The Long Term: Resisting Life Sentences, Working Toward Freedom.*

Beth E. Richie is head of the Department of Criminology, Law and Justice and professor of Black studies at the University of Illinois at Chicago. Richie is the author of *Compelled to Crime: the Gender Entrapment of Black Battered Women* and *Arrested Justice: Black Women, Violence and America's Prison Nation* and a coeditor of *The Long Term: Resisting Life Sentences, Working Toward Freedom.*